DISCOVERING
THE LOST
PYRAMID

G. Cope Schellhorn

Books by G. Cope Schellhorn

EXTRATERRESTRIALS IN BIBLICAL PROPHECY
and the New Age Great Experiment

Published by Horus House Press, Inc.

DISCOVERING THE LOST PYRAMID

G. Cope Schellhorn

HORUS HOUSE PRESS, INC.
MADISON, WISCONSIN
distributed to the trade by
INNER LIGHT PUBLICATIONS
NEW BRUNSWICK, NEW JERSEY

Library of Congress Catalog Card Number: 90-82716
ISBN: 0-938294-93-8

First Edition
First printing September 1990

Published by
Horus House Press, Inc.
P. O. Box 55185
Madison, Wisconsin 53705

Distributed by
Inner Light Publications
P. O. Box 753
New Brunswick, New Jersey 08903

Cover Art by Vicki Khuzami

Printed by
Litho Printers
Cassville, Missouri

For Rudolf,
a true Mason,
and his
wife, Jewell

Author's Note

Not long ago a man who wishes to remain anonymous appeared at my door. We had spoken together previously two days earlier by telephone. At that time he indicated to me he had a story which he wished to relate to someone who was a writer. Alas, I thought, he has chosen me.

Although I do not usually agree to listen to the tales of complete strangers, something about the man was different, very different. I could tell that much during our first conversation which was quite brief at that.

Now I found myself listening to a most remarkable story told by a most remarkable man. After hearing him out, I agreed almost immediately, which still surprises me when I think about it, to write his story. My mysterious friend maintained that everything I was told is true. Well, I can testify that I have checked it out as thoroughly as possible and can find no discrepancies in it anywhere. I have named my mysterious friend Yehneh, at his own request, and the story I have related is his almost word for word except that I have changed the first person pronoun to third person and done a bit of minor editing. The preface itself was written by Yehneh himself. I have not changed one word.

Yehneh's Preface

Long ago near the Great Pyramid of Giza, initiation Temple of the White Brotherhood, were buried the ancient records which are often spoken of as the records of the Lost Pyramid. It is the wish of the Brotherhood that these records now be brought forth to the light of day, that mankind in its spiritual development may better see where it is heading by becoming more aware of where it has been. Who, then, is so bold and spiritually hungry as to make the quest? And who so worthy as to succeed?

It is true that man has very little understanding of his earthly history and his relationship to his Creator, his cosmic neighbors and his fellow man. Much is to be found within the records which will help reorient mankind historically, and much is to be gained spiritually by the quest for them. The records have been looked after by the White Brotherhood for over twelve thousand years. It has been the honor of the Brotherhood, and one of its functions, to maintain these records until the time came when it was appropriate that they should come out into the light of day.

Now that time has come. Man has moved as far into the physical as he shall go. He must now choose between two alternatives, the gross physical or a movement upward. For those who choose the latter, it is a momentous uplifting into a greater enlightenment of being the value of which the individual and the race as a whole can hardly overestimate. The choice is, after all, an inevitable one that every individual spirit must make sooner or later. But now an old age is ending and a New Age has begun. The moment is ripe. The opportunity at hand. "Ask, and it shall be given you; seek, and ye shall find; knock, and it shall be opened unto you."

As a man develops, he has placed before him, in one way or another, in one form or another, the knowledge he needs which will further his spiritual growth. He must be able and willing to recognize the moment, reach out and take into himself the sustenance which will nurtur him and assuage his spiritual hunger. Though he may be spiritually ravenous, the food he finds teaches him universal compassion and the inextricable interrelatedness of all things.

It is the duty of the Brotherhood to contribute continuously to man's nurturing. Let no man claim that he is ignorant because he was not told or did not see. Each must seek. Each must reach out. God loves those who make the effort. He makes available to even the dimmest seeking soul, the bright eyes to see through the various darknesses which surround us all.

Most of what the public has come to consider "secret knowledge" isn't secret at all. The twelve Brotherhoods are making an increasingly greater effort to make available to all men everywhere the knowledge which has often been in their safekeeping—until the moment came, if I may paraphrase scripture here, when the babe need not be sopped with milk but was ready to be nurtured as a fully responsible, mature being.

The promise that the late President Anwar Sadat of Egypt gave to begin building a temple at the base of Mount Sinai fulfilled prophecy. It will not be a long wait now. The Creator brings his children to be united, and the Mount Sinai Temple, and the rebuilt Temple in Jerusalem, will both be fitting monuments to universal brotherhood.

Not very long ago a man and his wife were walking in the nave of Sitt Miriam (The Church of al Muallaga) which can be found in the old Coptic section of Cairo. It dates from the 4th century and is one of the oldest Christian churches in the world, sitting itself on the foundation of the old Roman Fort of Babylon. The man turned to the Coptic priest and said,

"Are you Egyptian?"

"Yes," he said, "I'm an Arab but Christian."

"And my wife and I are Jews. And here we are in an Arab country in a Christian church talking to an Arab Christian. It's as it should be. We're all brothers and shouldn't forget it. It's really so simple.''

True enough. We are all Sons of the Creator. Through Him we became the sons of Shem and Japheth and Ham. As Sons we are Brothers in our Father. It was never intended that we should live in disharmony, to doubt our Creator, our neighbors and our very selves. Let us move forward, then, and upward, guided by the memory of where we have been so that we may see more clearly where we must go. The alternative is too unappealing to be acceptable. And let us always remember as we go, that it is in the questing itself that lies the greatest reward, the greater growth. The objective of our quest, strangely, marvellously seems to recede before our eyes and is replaced, most appropriately, and in good and proper time, by a larger vision, a promise of even greater understanding as we continue to grow apace.

Yehneh

1

It was the beginning of light. Already the cool night air had been dimly brightened in the East as Yehneh walked the asphalt road on the north side of the Great Pyramid, passed the north entrance and continued on, following the shadowed road on the east side where the great sheet of limestone descended abruptly into the Nile Valley. Soon, he knew, the sun with rose-tipped fingers would be lifting itself over the lip of the world. He wanted to be where he could see it rise clearly.

In many ways this was the most important morning of his life. He looked upward and saw the last stars of morning holding brightly over the Pyramid. Then he stuck his hands deep in his pockets to warm them. The cold air had immediately brought his senses keenly alive. He watched his warm breath fog as it touched the crisp air around him. He was happy. He had awakened especially early for this. In fact, he had come six thousand miles to keep a promise and he had done so. He felt thankful and pleased, grateful but awed.

The Arab appeared almost out of nowhere, was suddenly there beside him, talking, friendly and persistent, mistaking him perhaps for a tourist. They walked together toward the slope, where the road cut down past the Sphinx into the valley, where the river thousands of years before had run close by, snug and green, near the great temple. Now it was out of sight, changing its course with the millennia, always the same yet not the same, feeding the people as they had come and gone through time. And the Great Temple had stood, always the same, waiting, a marker of what had been, what was and what would be, deathless in its stone symbolism, proclaiming the Glory of God to both the initiated and the uninitiated alike.

They took a seat together on a ledge of rock where they could look to the East. Below them, to the right, the great Sphinx lay in shadows, silently marking time, guarding in stone the Gates of Amenti, the afterlife, solidly and patiently awaiting its Masters to the end of time.

Above the horizon walked Venus. Yehneh could not remember her looking so large and bright and prepossessing. She moved slowly in the new light like a young maiden, white and flushed, come to celebrate the new day of her Father. And as the sky grew brighter, chasing the shadows, she seemed to step back, to recede, as the Father of Light moved boldly into his rightful place. She then withdrew herself, slowly, respectfully, in rhythm with her Father's advance, having done her duty and announced with her own soft light the splendour which is His alone.

Yehneh looked out over the valley toward this ancient symbol of the Cosmic

Light and he thanked God that he was there, that he had made this journey safely, that he had, he hoped, pleased his Creator, faithfully served the Brotherhood and kept his vows. He was more aware then than he had ever been before of how interrelated are the pieces of the Creator's work. He was alive again, born up by currents of love so great and overwhelming that words ended where thankfulness began.

He had come six thousand miles as a messenger of the Brotherhood to help raise the records of Thoth, God willing. He had worried greatly at times that he was not worthy, that along the way, like the proverbial sheep, he had become separated and lost, got so far diverted from the truth of things that others would have to go on without him. He knew that when the moment came the ancient archives of the Lost Pyramid would be given to the world. He also knew that where one fails others are always there to continue. Yet with all his heart he wanted to be a part of that enterprise. He wanted to please his Creator. He wanted to be found worthy.

- - - - -

This, then, is the story of the discovering of the ancient records of the Lost Pyramid, collected by the Sons of the Law of One and the "Seven Fingers" of Ra-Ta, buried by Thoth (Hermes) in the year 10,096 B.C. and watched over by the White Brotherhood since that day. This is a relation of how the moment came when the Creator assented, through the Brotherhood, to the raising of the records. This is also the story of Yehneh, one soul who symbolizes many, who, because of the great love of Him who created All, was found worthy to contribute his effort to the greater effort and to share in the great joy of attempting to uncover some of the ancient knowledge that the world now needs to see more clearly where it has been, so that it may see more clearly where it must go.

2

Yehneh looked out over the valley of the Nile and smiled. It was true he had come a long distance, and he had stumbled badly several times and had got up and continued on, because fulfilling his vows, he had come to realize, was more important than anything else. By doing so, he would be serving God and his fellow man and, not least, he would be enlightening himself out of the darkness.

It was several years ago that he and his wife had opened a door that led to a hall that ended in a temple. One night he had relaxed his body, lay back, put his mind into a trance and let her question him. They had never done this sort of thing before, and he was surprised at how

7

quickly he had gone into a deep hypnotic trance, how easily it had all happened. They had decided to try to explore the idea of former lives, if they indeed existed, and he had got much more than he expected.

He had projected out of his body to a century ago in Germany when he had been a law student in love with a young woman whose parents would not consent to their daughter marrying anyone who was not already established in business. Certainly not a student. This girl, whose name was Louise, had died of typhoid fever. He had that night a snapshot kaleidoscopic view of the relationship, and it had shook his emotions deeply. He had seen their first meeting at a dance, watched as they picnicked under a large hilltop tree in the breezes of summer, saw himself at the hospital room with the gift of a gold bracelet in his hand, heard her joke him for being such a serious fellow, saw her funeral, saw himself riding a horse, saw himself in fact returning to the hill of the long ago picnic, and then finally saw himself jerking the horse's reins fiercely, suddenly unable to go on, wishing desperately to turn the horse's head away, in another direction.

It was undeniably a very romantic story. And it all came bursting forth the first time he had regressed himself to another time. He found out that night that he had, indeed, had other lives. And that night changed his mind about so many things. It took him several weeks to recover from the emotional strain of it all. He would have to learn better to protect his emotions during succeeding sessions of that kind. There was so much to learn. He was immensely excited by what had happened yet waited several weeks before attempting another regression. In the meantime, something ever more significant was to happen. He was to meet, in a sense, his fate.

3

Several days after the German experience, he decided to try an additional experiment, although he was in no way consciously confident that anything much would come of it. He had read and heard of the idea that we all have "guides," guardian angels was the traditional Christian way of putting it. He had several times earlier conceived of the idea of trying to communicate, to go into trance and order his projected astral body to seek out his "guide," wherever this guide might be keeping himself. Each time he had considered trying the experiment, for one reason or another, he had put it off.

But one night he did not put it off. He propped himself up against the headboard next to his sleeping wife, relaxed his body from feet to head, and, after twenty minutes of relaxation, after building up the strength of his ego outside of his body, after imagining it was a ball of light getting heavier and heavier with energy, brighter and brighter with light, more and more concentrated with his essential being—finally, when he felt that he was thoroughly outside himself, hovering four inches above his own head, he commanded his etheric body to seek his guide, wherever he might be.

And nothing happened. He was not even sure he believed anything would happen. He brought himself back to the surface of consciousness and was almost ready to quit. But he did not quit. He decided to try once more.

Several moments after projecting himself out of his body, commanding his etheric body to seek out his guide, a wonderful thing happened.

Yehneh saw a man sitting in space on a two-seat, Shaker-like chair. He could distinctly see the spindles of the chair's back supporting the back of the man as he stretched casually with his legs and feet sticking straight out before him, as one might slouch in a physician's waiting room. The man seemed, in fact, to be waiting. He was dressed in slacks and a blue and white striped pullover. His facial complexion was swarthy, somewhat blemished, and he had black hair cut into bangs across the forehead.

Yehneh could see him clearly in that Shaker-like seat. Then the man spoke to him, and he would never forget his first words but years later would recall them with humor and deep affection.

The man said, ''My, what a heavy head.''

That was probably the best thing he could have said to him. It relaxed him, made everything seem less strange, more human.

And then there were several moments of hideous racket, as if great waves of cosmic interference had suddenly intervened to spoil the moment. Yehneh sensed the maliciousness of it and said,

''What's that?''

''Ignore it,'' the man said.

"Do I know you? Have I known you?"

"Yes."

And now Yehneh in his great excitement forgot to ask him where they had known one another, in what life, what land.

"Will you talk to me again in the future?"

"Yes."

"I'm not imagining this because I want to?"

"No." The voice seemed gentle, friendly, warmly amused.

"Will I be able to reach you when I want to?"

"Yes."

"What's your name? Do you mind if I ask?"

"No. It's Hotep."

"Thank you."

And later Yehneh would learn how the negative energies and impulses would attempt to divert this type of cosmic communication. He would learn to block out these negative energies, to concentrate his own positive thoughts on their destination and not give new energy to negativity by taking notice of it. He needed to learn so much, he knew, and even then in all his excitement, if he had known the mistakes he would make along the way, he would have been appalled at himself, ashamed to his very depths.

But that night was a great night. He had broken through, when he wasn't even consciously convinced it was possible. He was excited. It was, after all, a great moment. He awakened his wife and told her everything, and she said she was happy for him and not at all surprised and immediately returned to her dreams.

4

The next day Yehneh was irritated that in his excitement he had not asked more questions. There was so much he wanted, needed to know about tangible and intangible things.

He wanted to ask more questions. Who was this Hotep? He looked Indian, perhaps Aztec. No, he decided, the name and the haircut, the swarthy complexion made him more Egyptian.

He got on the telephone and called the Egyptology Department of one of the nation's great universities. He wondered, with questions like his, if they wouldn't think he was joking or worse still, mentally unbalanced. Yet when he explained who he was, that he had gone into a trance state and had spoken to an entity, to a ''man'' who had called himself Hotep, and then asked, did that particular name have meaning? the answer he received was reassuring.

The Egyptologist said yes, it did. It meant ''gift'' but was used mainly in conjunction with other things.

''Ask him what else his name is,'' he said politely.

And Yehneh had rushed to put himself into a relaxed state, rushed to put himself into a trance. He tried very hard to visualize Hotep's facial features and project to him. He was not disappointed. The entity was waiting, just as he promised he would be.

''Is there more to your name?'' he asked him.

''It doesn't matter,'' he was told.

''That isn't all of your name then?''

''It really doesn't matter.''

''Do you mind if I ask anyway?''

''No.''

''What is it then?''

''Amenhotep...''

An emotional rush of excitement had

come over Yehneh, and he did not hear everything clearly.

"Did you say Amenhotep the Third?"

"Amenhotep the Fourth," the man replied. "Ikhnaton, the king."

Yehneh was extremely excited. He could hardly control the surges of emotion boiling up within him.

"We knew each other?"

"Yes."

"When you were pharaoh?"

"Yes, I was your friend."

And that was about all he could handle for one day. So much was happening so fast that he needed time to psychologically digest the significance of the things he was learning.

There were so few people he could confide in. Mostly he talked to his wife and his friend Johnstone.

When he mentioned several days later to Johnstone the fact that he had broken through to his "guide" and told him who his guide was, his friend, who was wise in many things, thought for a moment and said,

"Ask him if Ikhnaton was one of the earlier lives of Jesus. It has been suggested as a possibility before now."

And Yehneh, standing with his friend, had asked on the very spot they stood. And the answer had been dizzying. He felt blessed but confused. There was so much he didn't understand.

His friend had not seemed surprised at all.

5

In the following weeks Yehneh found it necessary to do what his friend said he would have to do. He had to discard eighty percent of the knowledge he had accumulated over the years. So much of what he thought was true, and what had been taught to him as truth, was turning out to be not true at all. The shock to his nervous system became almost unbearable.

He had to begin anew, build a way of looking at the world quite differently from the way he had perceived it in the past. It was the same world but it was surely not the same world. Sometimes he felt like he had just arrived on earth and had been tossed unceremoniously into a new culture and a new way of living.

If it had not been for Hotep who, as he had promised, was always willing to answer questions, to guide his new protégé into this new world, and his wife and his friend Johnstone, he could not have stood the strain. There were moments when he slipped into the deepest despair. At times he felt completely unworthy, as if now greater expectations had been put upon him, heaped upon him, he who slogged along so miserably in the marshes of his ignorance and weak will, like some lame duck that had lost the webbing down in the foundation parts to keep him afloat and propel him along.

And as he began to understand more the purpose that was gradually being made clear to him, he had moments of fright and stupidity that embarrassed him greatly. He felt like the most fortunate being and the most inept fool, and at times he almost cried out to God, "Oh, I'm not ready for this. What do you expect of me?"

Hotep was always there to steady him, to convince him that the past in a man's life was not important, or only marginally so; that what mattered was making the attempt to understand the moment and having the will power to put a foot forward in a sincere effort to shape the future into a better world. That could be done by using this new, more accurate knowledge he was learning.

Yehneh began to understand that if a human being really wishes to know the creation about him, his place in it, and even the Creator Himself, his eyes will be gradually opened at a pace commensurate with the level of his present development and his capacity to digest the truth. That is as it has been and always shall be. It is the great promise of abiding Light within darkness, he was told.

6

It is not surprising, then, that it was several months before Yehneh was ready to learn more about his relationship with Hotep in the life he had referred to in one of their first conversations.

One warm spring evening Yehneh stretched out comfortably on the living room sofa and put himself into a trance. He had put a tape recorder close by which his wife could turn on as soon as she began to ask him questions. They had made a list of questions that they both thought were pertinent, and he told her to ask any others that came to mind during the regression itself.

Then he directed his astral body,

whose energy he had collected into a bright light several inches above his head, to obey the suggestions of his wife and to answer her questions accordingly:

Q. I want you to go back in time to a former Egyptian life during the reign of I k h n a t o n .
(Long pause.) Upon awakening, you will remember all the details. I'm going to count to three and I want you to tell me where you are. I want you to view this life without emotion. One... two...three...Where are you? (Long pause.)
A. I see the picture of the pyramid of Hept Supht (the Great Pyramid).
Q. What is your name?
A. Hoshi.
Q. Is Hoshi your full name?
A. No. Hoshi Ahk-Tuk.
Q. Where in Egypt do you come from?
A. Lower Egypt.
Q. What are your parents' names?
A. Sulit...Ben Amun.
Q. Do you have any brothers?

A. I have one brother.

Q. What is his name?

A. Not sure...

Q. Do you have any sisters?

A. (No response.)

Q. What education? Are you in school?

A. I went to priest schools.

Q. Did you choose to go to priest schools?

A. No. My father sent me.

Q. Did you want to go?

A. Yes.

Q. How long were you in school? How many years?

A. Fifteen years.

Q. You studied fifteen years to become a priest?

A. Yes.

Q. I want you to describe the first meeting with the pharaoh, the first time you saw the pharaoh.

A. (Long pause.) He is sitting on a throne. He says "Come here, boy."

Q. What is the pharaoh's name? (Long pause. Subject very emotional.) I want you to view this without emotion.

What is the pharaoh's name?

A. It is the new pharaoh, Ikhnaton.

Q. Were you in school studying to be a priest the first time you saw him?

A. Yes.

Q. When you finished your education you were then a priest, at the end of your education?

A. Yes.

Q. What were your duties as a priest?

A. My duties were to maintain the temple.

Q. And as a priest, what was your relationship with the pharaoh?

A. I was a priest.

Q. Did you know his wife?

A. Yes.

Q. What was his wife's name?

A. Nefertitti.

Q. What was the political situation in Egypt at that time?

A. There are riots in the streets. Much fighting. The pharaoh doesn't seem to be bothered...very calm. He calls me to him.

Q. What does he want when he calls

you to him?

A. Asks me to help him stop the fighting.

Q. Were you able to help stop the fighting?

A. No, but I try. He asks me...he asks me to be his Nunca.

Q. To be his Nunca?

A. To be head of the other priests.

Q. And you accept?

A. Yes.

Q. What is the religious situation in Egypt at this time?

A. I don't like it. Many of the priests don't like it. The pharaoh has changed things so much.

Q. Where did he get the idea of one God and why did he support it?

A. He is God...God gave him the idea. But he is God.

Q. Did you support him enough?

A. I loved him. He was honest and good. He was pure.

Q. Were you friends with the other priests?

A. Some priests.

Q. Are any of them alive today?

A. Many.

Q. Would you tell me some of their names?

A. I work with them. Many of the people. I work with priests and priestesses.

Q. Your friend Johnstone, was he a priest?

A. He was a priest.

Q. What was his name?

A. Tertti.

Q. What was your relationship?

A. ...Tertti Ahk Eben.

Q. What was your relationship?

A. He was my friend.

Q. He was your friend?

A. He was a good man. He helped me. When I was a boy studying, he helped me.

Q. Was he older than you?

A. A little bit...Three years older. He helped me with my school work.

Q. I want you to go to the time when you first met me and describe the time.

A. (Long pause.) I'm not sure.

Q. Where are you?

A. I'm not sure. She comes from a

family in Thebes.

Q. What is my name?

A. (Long pause.) They call you Notti.

Q. Is that my full name?

A. Notti Ebeni...Notti Ebeni.

Q. When did you first see Notti?

A. I'm not sure. I think in the street at the market place. I think she was buying fruits and vegetables.

Q. Was Notti a priestess then?

A. No. I asked her if she would like to be a priestess and she said she would like to be. I had her sent to school. She was very beautiful.

Q. Were you a priest when you first met Notti?

A. Yes.

Q. How old were you then?

A. I was twenty-three years old. I was not the Nunca.

Q. How old was Notti?

A. Eighteen.

Q. Notti attended school prior to that?

A. Notti attended school, yes. She was a very good student.

Q. As a priest, were you able to be with the priestesses in school?

A. What?

Q. Do the priestesses attend school at the temple?

A. Yes.

Q. So as a priest, you were able to see the priestesses attending school?

A. I watched her study. I liked her. She watched me out of the corner of her eye. She always liked me.

Q. Where did the priests live?

A. The priests lived in the temple.

Q. Where did the priestesses live?

A. The students lived at home. The priestesses lived in the temple, in a part of the temple.

Q. How long does it take to become a priestess?

A. Six years...to become a full priestess. I helped you with your work. I wanted you to pass initiation. Tertti laughs at me. He thinks it's all very funny.

Q. Why does Tertti think it's funny?

A. That I help you with your school work.

Q. What do the initiations of the priests and priestesses consist of?

A. To swear obedience to Aton and the pharaoh. They bow before the pharaoh, all the priests and priestesses on their knees and bow their heads. There were many, many new priests for the new pharaoh.

Q. Many new priestesses?

A. You became a priestess when you were twenty-seven. Many of the older ones left. They did not like the new pharaoh. He's in good humor. He jokes...he makes jokes sometimes with the priestesses during the ceremony. He's very glad. He's very—I see all the priestesses in a row before him bowing on their knees with their heads down.

Q. What are the priestesses wearing?

A. They are wearing white robes, very long with white tassels.

Q. What do the priests wear?

A. I wear gray. I wear gray.

Q. Do you wear a robe?

A. Yes.

Q. Why do you wear a gray robe?

A. Because I am the Nunca.

Q. And what color do the other priests wear?

A. Black.

Q. Are you the only Nunca?

A. Yes. I had just been appointed the Nunca when you were becoming a priestess.

Q. Was there a Nunca before you?

A. Yes.

Q. What happened to him?

A. Nothing.

Q. Is he still serving the pharaoh?

A. No. He did not like the new pharaoh's God. He asked to be excused from service.

Q. What was his name?

A. Rahota.

Q. Did you know him?

A. Not very well.

Q. Do you know him today?

A. No.

Q. I want to know the significance of the anhk.

A. The anhk is life.

Q. As a priest did you wear an anhk?

A. Sometimes. Most of the time.

Q. The anhk signifies life?

A. Yes, in all its facets. In all its beauty and all its diversity.

Q. What was the significance of the lotus?

A. The lotus is perfection. And life...and life everlasting.

Q. Did you wear a lotus? As a piece of jewelry did you wear a lotus?

A. No.

Q. Did anyone wear a lotus?

A. Some...liked a lotus.

Q. As a priest, did you make jewelry?

A. Yes.

Q. Who did you make jewelry for?

A. We used it to wear in the religious ritual. It's beautiful. It's both beautiful and practical.

Q. You made jewelry for yourself?

A. Oh, yes.

Q. Did you make jewelry for others?

A. Yes, but not when I was Nunca. But I watched.

Q. What metals did you use?

A. Gold, bronze, copper...all kinds of metals and all kinds of gems.

Q. Were you able to cut the stones

yourself?

A. No. But some could.

Q. Jewelry was made at the temple?

A. Yes.

Q. What metal was particularly important to you?

A. Gold. Gold is important to everyone. It is the sun...the perfect metal.

Q. Did you know Gloria in that lifetime? What was her name?

A. Yes.

Q. What was her name?

A. Suki...Suki.

Q. What was your relationship?

A. She was a priestess. She was very haughty.

Q. She was what?

A. Haughty. She liked me. She did not like you. She was jealous.

Q. Why was she jealous of me?

A. Because you loved me and were my favorite.

Q. Did you love me?

A. Very much.

Q. How long did you serve as a priest under the pharaoh?

A. Twelve years...twelve years.

Q. What happened toward the end of Ikhnaton's reign?

A. There was still fighting. They were lying...some of the old priests that had quit with the wealthy...some of the wealthy people in town.

Q. I want you to rise above this and view it without emotion. I want you to describe how you were betrayed and who betrayed you.

A. It was hard to tell...very hard to tell. So many people pretended to support the pharaoh and lied. I never knew. Even some of the priestesses and priests were lying. They pretended to support him and they didn't really, Tertti says.

Q. Tertti support him?

A. Yes.

Q. Did Notti support him?

A. Yes.

Q. Did Suki support him?

A. (Pause.) She lied. She said the pharaoh was born malformed because the gods were angry. She lied.

Q. So there were many who betrayed you, some you did know and some you didn't know?

A. Yes.

Q. What happened after that?

A. We were executed.

Q. Do you know who executed you?

A. Rema.

Q. What is the name?

A. His name was Rema.

Q. Do you know this person today?

A. Yes, I know him.

Q. Do you know where you were executed, in what city?

A. Ikhetaton. Rema was an old priest who had quit, and they plotted and schemed. (Pause.) She was his lover.

Q. Who was his lover?

A. Suki.

Q. Suki was his lover so she helped him?

A. She was angry at me.

Q. Why was she angry at you?

A. Because of you. You did not like her. None of the priestesses liked her. She was snobby and aloof and haughty. You said someone should shave her head and laughed—cut all her hair off.

Q. Did we cut her hair off?

A. No. That someone should cut all

of her hair off.

Q. I want to take you to the last day of your life. I want you to view this without emotion and rise above it and describe it. (Pause.) Where are you?

A. Ah, in Ikhetaton. They took us out, stood us in rows, all the priests who supported the pharaoh.

Q. How many priests are there?

A. Seventy-three..seventy-three priests from the temple.

Q. Where's the pharaoh?

A. He's dead. They killed him.

Q. How long ago did they kill him?

A. Couple of days. That's what they say.

Q. What about the pharaoh's children?

A. I don't know what happened to them.

Q. What were the chldren's names?

A. Tut...son-in-law...

Q. Will Tut become the new pharaoh or will they kill him, too?

A. I don't like him. He's weak.

Q. Tut?

A. He's weak and too young. He's a

spoiled boy. I don't like his father to know that I don't like him.

Q. Do you like Nefertitti?

A. Yes. Everyone likes Nefertitti. She is gentle and wise and very beautiful.

Q. What's happened to Nefertitti?

A. I don't know.

Q. Without emotion tell me what happened the last day of your life.

A. They lined us up, three lines and...then they chopped our heads off. They chopped my head off first.

Q. Because you were high priest?

A. Because I was Nunca.

Q. What did they do with the bodies?

A. Put them in a pit and covered them with sand. Rema was there...he was there.

Q. Do you know what happened to Notti?

A. She became a slave.

Q. Viewing your life from spirit, what lessons did you learn?

A. I learned you cannot trust what people say. It's what they do...that counts. Some people smile with hate in their minds and others look sad and are truly happy. You have to be able to look into their minds and you cannot always do that. (Pause.) I learned to trust the pharaoh. He was a great king.

Q. Did you see him in spirit life?

A. Many times.

Q. What in that lifetime was of most value to mankind?

A. The pharaoh is a lesson of love. They are all so busy. They did not like their lives changed. They did not like change.

Q. I want you to remember everything. I want you to awaken.

7

Yehneh became awakened in body and spirit and began to remember more and more. The days went by rapidly as his understanding began to increase. He read the Books of the Masters and the Books of the Messengers. He went to the Egyptian *Book of the Coming Out into Light* (often erroneously referred to as the *Book of the Dead),* to the *Emerald Tablets,* to the *Kabala,* especially the *Zohar*, that ancient book of wisdom which even the Jews themselves seem to have forgotten. He read the *Bhagavad-Gita*, the Old and New Testaments, and many of the suppressed books of the Gnostics.

He found that he was led from one book to another, that at moments they fused, told one story. He learned that what was superficial was pyrite, and that the real gold, the truth, was often found several veins deeper in the matrix. What one could render out of that level often went far beyond the literal meaning of the surface. If the standard definition of irony is when the actual meaning is just the opposite of the literal meaning, then Yehneh realized, much of the knowledge that has been preserved, saved from destruction, has been passed along in texts that are very ironical. This was done not to obfuscate the mind of the student, the true seeker, but to protect the material from the slash of the censor's stroke and the fire of the book burner. Thus those reams of esoteric symbolism and emblemism that at first glance often seem so difficult and silly.

He also learned that as one grew in spirit, his eyes brightened and he began to see more clearly. And he knew the opposite was true as well. If one refused to learn, one grew duller, more blind. Yet there never seemed to be enough light. "More light, Father," he would pray. "Please, I need more light if I am to understand." These words became almost a continuous prayer.

One evening he was reading Ruth Montgomery's *The World Before* when he came across for the first time the legend (most still say myth) that ancient records telling of earlier world history, the history of Lemuria and Atlantis, and of the early founding and settling of the land of Khem (Egypt) were buried in the vicinity of the Great Pyramid. The feeling he had at that moment was peculiar. Extraordinary. Without having asked his new guide, he knew that he knew. A great wave of nervous energy came over him. He called out to his wife and told her, expecting her to look at him doubtfully. But she did not.

"I know where they are buried," he said. "I helped bury them."

"Why don't you ask your guide. I'm sure he'll help you."

And he did ask and was told, yes, he knew where the records were buried. Yes, he had helped collect and bury them.

And in this way he discovered his greatest vow. He had promised the Elder Brothers that upon incarnating, if it were the will of God and the wish of the Brotherhood that had watched over them so long, he would find the records and help raise them to the light of day.

8

The next day he sat at his desk and dreamed. He could dimly see the records, see them being sequestered, buried, see them rising, being brought to the light of day to help mankind in this pivotal age to understand itself better. He knew how much mankind needed to come to understand its Creator, how much the records might help people, who were willing to look and to understand with unprejudiced eyes, trace the ancient history effectively so that it might be made to shed its light upon what kind of tomorrow we can expect if we insist on following the path of yesterday and today. There had been terrible mistakes made that had been avoidable. How many, he wondered, were willing to listen now and would be changed significantly in character if they had more accurate records of man's past?

He was sitting in his chair, swiveling this way and that when his friend Johnstone had walked in. Johnstone was his confidant, a fellow inquirer, a Brother, and he shared his life with him. He loved him for the help he had given him. He couldn't wait to speak.

"Johnstone," he said. "I've got something to tell you. I know where the records are buried, the ones by the Great Pyramid."

Johnstone was standing by the door. He smiled.

"I think I do, too."

"What?"

"I think I know, too. Ask your guide."

And Yehneh asked his guide and was told that yes, his friend also knew.

Yehneh would learn that they, the two of them, were the only mortals alive at that time who knew exactly where the sacred records were buried. They had come back, with the blessing of the Brotherhood, to find and help raise the records. But to do so they must find their way clearly to God's greater purpose. In some ways they were far more than just representatives of the Brotherhood. They were men, human beings subject to all the errors and folly that flesh gives birth to, and they represented all those human beings about them and all those who had preceded them. They must prove themselves ready and worthy of the task before them. They must help their fellow human beings claim that birthright offered by the Creator to all who progress through the material plane of existence until that grand moment, that glorious cosmic instant when they first recognize the truth of the great promise that has been made. Man need not die in spirit, the promise says. There is no death for those who claim the spark of the Creator within them and ask that they be allowed to continue to live selflessly in that spark, to help tender it and fan it into a blaze of glorious cosmic Light that abides forever, cycles of life and death within seemingly endless chains of being, and yet new life always greater and more glorious, separate and yet indivisible from the Creator, the great paradox that is no contradiction. Yehneh would learn that the raising of the records, their translation, interpretation and the dissemination of the information within them would help man become more aware of that promise. And that learning spurred him, drove him, yet invigorated him and sustained him.

He was also to begin to understand how much he had let his life slip from a path that could lead him to his vow. He began to find how easy and yet how seemingly difficult it is to put away destructive habits. How difficult it is to break old habits and patterns so that one might be "regenerated on the mount."

At times he gave in to the most abject despair. He would think that the world was abysmally polluted, that he himself was not worthy at all and would never be so. He knew that the Creator could ordain that the records be raised at any moment and that they would rise at that moment.

There was nothing immutably written anywhere that said that Johnstone and himself alone could cause the records to surface. That was ego, the grossest kind of vanity. They had been told that they had permission *to try to* raise the records. That was all. If they continued to please God and if the Brotherhood continued to have faith in them, then perhaps...

As time passed, he became especially aware of how many people were deeply involved in one way or another with the fate of the records. To get even the majority of these people working together in harmony at any time seemed almost hopeless. And to get them to do so seemed precisely the point, it seemed to him, as the days turned into months and the months passed into years.

Faith, faith. How hard it is for the brokenhearted in a world that teaches that only what is solid is what is real. He realized he had been passing in the wrong direction for years. And the years were going by, the earth and its life wave were moving toward a major climactic moment, one of those moral and physical turning points that the planet and its life forms experience every few thousand years. There was nothing indelibly written that said the records would be raised before that moment. And yet if it were possible, if it could be, then he hoped with all his heart, with the spark of God that still burned within him, that his friend and himself could qualify in their own way...to be of service.

9

Yet he made his own mistakes. He did not always believe as much as he needed to believe. At times he doubted, and he hated himself for doing so, and yet he doubted. Even with a special guide to guide him, the wonderful Master of Masters, he still doubted. If he failed with such a guide, then how could others, who were not so fortunate as to have direct communication with such an advanced spirit, then how, he wondered, did they stand much of a chance against the snares and pitfalls of this physical world? At times he almost let himself convince himself that he was quite mad, had become crazed within the act of living itself. And it was thoughts like those that sent him out searching several times seeking verification of what he had been already told.

It wasn't long before he found himself standing at a public Psychic Fair with a crowd of people interested in occult things just as he himself was. Perhaps they were in search of the same thing he was looking for—verification of a supernatural reality that they had begun to suspect even in a disbelieving world. Some perhaps wanted a quick glimpse into their future, to be the better prepared for tomorrow, to gain an edge. And some, he knew, came to find out about "things," about people they knew and wanted to know more about, about people they often distrusted. Some were sincerely concerned for their spiritual growth and were seeking direction, advice and companionship in their lives. The motives were surely as many as were the people. The place was the market place of Babylon West. The commodity for sale was the psychic talent of sidewalk seers and prophets.

Yehneh knew one must not sell his gift ever for a price, that it must be given freely, if it is to be given at all. But he did not know it well enough yet. He would learn. He would become convinced of the truth of the need for helping others with no thought of any kind of compensation. He would learn that cosmic law preceded the gift. It was the duty of the gift. The more gifted, the more responsible one becomes. It's that simple.

Yet there he stood. He would see, he thought. He would buy some verification.

He walked over to the table where the clairvoyant sat who specialized in "former lives." That was what he wanted. He stopped there.

She took him into the period of Ikhnaton. Much of what she said verified factually what he had been told by his guide and what he had learned from regressing himself. Oh, he thought at the time, it was worth it. She added details he did not know consciously. And she described the last days of the pharaoh's reign.

She told him that he had given the

pharaoh a draught of poison. It had been Ikhnaton's wish. He did not want to be captured and have his mind twisted in torture until he could be publically exhibited as an embarrassing spectacle and his mind and body possibly invaded and possessed by spirits other than his own. She described for him his own torture and that of his friends. It was very vivid stuff what she told him, how they had been hung up naked on hooks in the temple of Bast. She told him he had known how to leave his body and had done so soon, rising to hover in the ether, watching the grim ordeal below.

And later he would ask his guide about what she said, and he would verify the accuracy of it all for him. Yehneh seemed then to have no shame. He did not know enough at the time to realize that involuntary clairvoyants such as this one are not always accurate. And on the days when their gift is not working for them, some of them are not always truthful. When what comes out of your mouth has to do with what goes in, one is not always careful. An empty stomach can very easily salt an imagination.

Least of all, he was not thinking about the injunction against seeking out false prophets. He was looking for verification because he didn't trust himself to hear clearly. And he was guilty, as was Thomas, of doubting. It was a matter of faith. First he must trust the ability of the spark within him to reach out and touch directly all of creation at any given moment if necessary. He must learn to trust his ability to hear and see clearly. He must learn, in short, to know himself. His guide would tell him so again and again, but sometimes he didn't seem to hear. He was like a deaf, willful child. Again he doubted, and he hated himself for doubting, and yet he doubted.

He and his friend Johnstone met with the professional clairvoyant several times at her apartment. And Johnstone soon became overly influenced by the woman. They both began going to psychic sessions at her place that were also attended by several of her friends. Johnstone encouraged Yehneh to keep attending, and Yehneh gladly did so, at least in the beginning.

It was not that Yehneh finally decided that the woman was a totally negative person. But looking back now, he could see how her life served as the epitome of the misuse of God-given gifts to the detriment ultimately of herself and others around her. Early on he could see that she was interested in amassing and focusing psychic power against her enemies. She spoke of black magicians and sending back to them what they deserved. It was psychic eye for an eye with her.

By the second session Yehneh had begun to have doubts about what he was doing there. The woman spoke of forming a group which could have a positive effect on the community. She spoke of certain "good works" that needed to be accomplished. These "works" as far as he could make out involved using her powers to move things and manipulate people. He did not like what he had been learning.

When the woman spoke of manipulating a love match between

herself and a friend of Johnstone's, Yehneh began to withdraw. Even love was seen as a means to power. The man was well-to-do with a respectable position in public service. That the man was married mattered not a wit with her.

As far as knowledge of the sacred records was concerned, she knew some things. She maintained that she was the incarnation of Isis and that in time she herself would travel to Egypt and enter the record vault, there to take up the Caduseus of Thoth (Hermes) and wield new found power with this instrument. Wielding power, not raising and translating and disseminating the knowledge of the records for the benefit of mankind, was her intent. That was her game.

Yehneh, who in the beginning was convinced that she was one of those supposed to assist in the raising of the records, and had his own guide's word for that, began to have second thoughts. He had initially accepted the idea that she played a considerable part in things, especially after she passed along to Johnstone and himself the ancient *Emerald*

Tablets of Thoth. In this way she had carried out part of her vows. And he was not quite thankful to her for that. Receiving the *Tablets* at that time was crucially important to the project of raising the records.

As the woman slid deeper into the shadowed world of attempted psychic manipulation of others, he and Johnstone both decided they must break off further contact with her. They did so regrettably but knew it was necessary. Yehneh consulted with his guide and the decision was made. He was told that those who for one reason or another were unable to continue with the work at the present time, would be given future opportunities for service when they were more ready.

It is, as Yehneh was to learn over and over again, a very loving Creator, who is eternally ready to forgive those who love Him and seek Him.

10

Until now he had never regressed himself to the time of the sinking of the records into the subsurface vault in the vicinity of the Great Pyramid and of the raising of the Great Pyramid itself. He had questioned his guide and had received answers that had satisfied him. He had the information he needed at any given moment in time. What he needed, and what he was ready to receive, always seemed to be given to him at the proper time.

Now, he was told, would be a good time to regress himself back to that time, to ask a series of questions that needed to be asked. There was so much that he needed to know if his friend and himself were to contiue to work on retrieving the records.

He seated himself comfortably on his bed with his back against the backboard and his legs and feet spread out on the bedspread before him. Then he began to relax his body, focus his energy into his astral body and send it hurtling through the illusion of time.

His wife entered the room when he had reached a deep trance state. She sat down next to him and began with preparatory remarks which preceded questioning.

(The following transcription is an abridgement of a longer tape.)

Q. I am going to ask you some questions. You will answer them as best you can. You will remember later everything you say. I want you to send your mind back to the time of the building of the Great Pyramid. (Pause.) If you were alive then, let your thoughts return to a happy moment in that life. (Pause.) What do you see? (Pause.) How old are you?

A. 43.

Q. What is your name?

A. Threegee Sar Tana.

Q. Are you a full-blooded Egyptian?

A. No.

Q. Do you have any brothers or sisters?

A. Two sisters.

Q. Where are you from originally?

A. Urfina...Urfina—Atlantis.

Q. What was your father's occupation?

A. Metal worker in Atlantis.

Q. And your mother's?

A. Dancing girl.

Q. What is your occupation or position?

A. A priest.

Q. Where were you educated?

A. In the priest school for 15 years in Atlantis. An Egyptian 22 years. (Subject was a resident of Egypt 27 years.)

Q. Have you helped with the building of the Great Pyramid?

A. Yes. I helped lay the plans.

Q. Why was the Pyramid built?

A. For the glory of God.

Q. Who was responsible for the idea?

A. The king Arart was asked by Hermes.

Q. How were the large stones transported?

A. By a beam of light. And the river.

Q. How were the large stones cut and shaped?

A. A beam of light.

Q. How long did it take to build the Pyramid?

A. 22 years.

Q. Did you live close to the construction site?

A. No. In town.

Q. How did you get to the construction site each day?

A. Well, you can take a camel or walk or fly in a machine or go in your head.

Q. Could everyone go in their head?

A. No. Some of the priests can.

Q. How many workers were involved in the construction?

A. 500 to 1,000 of the king's people.

Q. Did the builders get help from outer space beings?

A. Yes. From Therga, a friend of Hermes.

Q. Where is Therga from?

A. Fourth star off the meridian.

Q. What kind of help?

A. How to raise stones?

Q. Will these outer space beings return?

A. Yes, maybe.

Q. Is there a sunken store of knowledge hidden near the Great Pyramid?

A. Yes.

Q. Without giving the location, is the knowledge within a structure that is buried?

A. Yes.

Q. Was the structure lowered into a shaft?

A. Yes.

Q. Please describe the shaft.

A. It is square, 20 feet by 22 feet and 206 feet deep straight down.

Q. How was the shaft constructed?

A. (Long pause.) Cut by heat, beam from the rod.

Q. How many workers worked to construct it?

A. 12 workers.

Q. What is the shape of the buried structure within which the knowledge may be found?

A. Pyramid, gold and hollow,

weighs 3,000 pounds. It is 18 feet by 12 feet with a chamber 5 feet square. Floor is airtight.

Q. Please describe generally what this knowledge is.

A. History of what happened to Atlantis...of the people...many tribes of Atlantis. So much is missing. In thin tablets of manganese metal. In three languages...a little of Lemurian, the language of Atlantis and the language of the king.

Q. Describe everything else to be found in the shaft.

A. Twelve bodies (The twelve workers.) Tert and Trimis. (The two guardians. Their real names have been changed.) Four boxes in corners. Clothing and jewelry. Names. The firestick. The crystal. Parts of the airship Volanda.

Q. Is this structure to be located soon?

A. Yes.

Q. By whom?

A. Horta and me.

Q. Why?

A. The Masters want it to be found. Otherwise people will do it all over again.

Q. Did Hermes Trismegistus (Thoth) have much to do with the knowledge buried there and the construction of the shaft?

A. He talked the king into building the shaft.

Q. What was Ra-Ta's relationship to the project?

A. He was high priest of the Temple of God.

Q. How long did it take to dig the shaft and bury the records?

A. Five years.

Q. Who was the king?

A. Arart.

Q. What was the relationship of Horta, now known as Johnstone, to the project?

A. Chief engineer. Ra-Ta's most trusted priest.

Q. Are there entities now guarding the structure?

A. Yes.

Q. What are their names?

A. Tert and Trimis.

Q. Did your soul mate work on the construction of the shaft?

A. Yes. As a stonemason. Hermes

told me. His name was Heraneous.

Q. What happened to him?

A. Died. Took poison. All the workers took poison.

Q. Did you use an airship to bring documents from Atlantis to the project?

A. Yes.

Q. What year was the shaft sunk?

A. 10,096 B.C.

Q. Did Donald Q. aid in the enterprise?

A. Yes. Anana.

Q. Who else aided in the project?

A. Seven Fingers of Ra-Ta.

Q. Ra-Ta had seven fingers?

A. No.

Q. Who were the Seven Fingers of Ra-Ta?

A. Horta, Anee, Wayo, Eka, Hera, Hiyo...(Rest of answer could not be clearly heard.)

Q. Move now in time to the day of your death. How did it happen?

A. Plane crashed. It was an old machine. Hera was with me.

Q. What did you learn from this life?

A. That life is so much work and so

much responsibility.

He came out of the trance remembering everything. As long as his wife gave him the suggestion to remember everything that transpired during the session, he would do so. It often surprised him how mistaken the average person's idea of the trance state and hypnosis is. There are, of course, some significant variations as to technique and subject reaction from one situation to another. He did not wish to pose as an expert, but he did realize that the effective use of hypnosis to benefit society and the individual at the present stage of human development was in its dark ages.

He knew that by autosuggestion he was able to reach a fairly deep state of hypnosis. He also knew when he was hypnotized. At the same time that he was aware of being questioned, at the moment when he was Yehneh sitting on the bed and aware that he was hypnotized, being questioned, aware even of the questioner's identity and of the background noises that could be so disturbing—at the very same time he was someone else in a life that seemed to long antedate the present moment. He would answer questions as if he were in that faraway life, living it at that moment, or at least as if he were standing before it, watching it appear before his eyes like images on a movie screen or computer scanner.

He was then really two people at once—the hypnotized subject aware of his hypnosis and the "historical" subject under investigation. It never ceased to fascinate him, this infinitely comprehensive creation of the Godhead known as Man. How little he understood of it, he thought. How fantastical yet real this life current that has no discernible beginning, no beginning time, no end time. And how we plod along day by day insistently living by the wristwatch, as if we are marking something definite, as if we can pinpoint and pinch to our specifications those humdrum material designs we cherish so fiercely and bend so everlastingly within the eternal force currents of the cosmos. How we limit ourselves by keeping our vision earthbound, when we could share more fully in the cosmic vision if we looked skyward more often and developed a sense of loving curiosity toward all the cosmic forces and their Creator and Sustainer.

11

From this time on, Yehneh and John-stone began to actively seek support for the project in the material world. Yehneh came to realize that although the Creator could raise Himself the records any time at His will, and although the Elder Brothers working through the Creator could raise up the records at will, it was the wish of the Creator and Elder Brothers that man, who had buried much of his own early history for safekeeping, should come, working in harmony in the physical plane, to retrieve the records of his own past. The Creator and the Elder Brothers would shepherd him and give him their active support when he was spiritually and mentally and physically ready.

To accomplish this great task, however, man must remember. He must exercise his will properly. Just how ready he must be, and in what way, not even Yehneh fully understood. The day would come when he understood better, and it would not be far in the future, and when that day did come, he would be awed standing before his Creator. He would never cease to be totally awed by the Creator and His words from that day on. Not ever.

Yehneh and Johnstone were advised to send a letter of inquiry to the Egyptology Department of a great Midwestern university, addressed to the same Egyptologist who had spoken to Yehneh in the past, which now seemed so long ago, and had explained to him the meaning of the word *hotep*. They wrote together the following letter:

Dear Professor X and Fellow Members,

What we come to you with may seem extraordinary to your conscious mind.

74

To your subconscious mind it will make great sense, we hope. Mr. Johnstone and I write to you as we have been directed. Separately and with a certain amazement initially, we have been contacted by the guides from the other side of physical consciousness. We have been told of the location of what will become the most important archeological find in recorded time.

To be specific: buried near the Great Pyramid of Giza is a small perservative pyramid eighteen by twelve feet in dimension. This pyramid was specially constructed to hold the spiritual, philosophical and technical history of the "lost" continents of Lemuria and Atlantis. This gold covered pyramid contains a chamber five feet square in which the information will be found.

It is with humility that we come to you with this knowledge. We have been told to approach you and are most willing to lead your archeologists to the designated spot which, with some simple tests, will reveal the substantiality of the pyramid itself.

We will be waiting to hear from you, certain, as we have been told, that the time has come for such an enterprise to be accomplished.

Sincerely,

Professor X was also contacted by telephone and told about the tape recording concerning the records. He indicated he would be interested in listening to it.

On a cold winter day, one of the coldest of the winter of '78, Yehneh and his friend drove through a blizzard and met the professor in his warm office. It was a congenial meeting. The man said little but listened intently. He asked few questions but told the two of them that he found what they had brought him very interesting and, although his department was not working on projects in that part of Egypt and did not have the permission of the Egyptian government to do so, he would give them the address of a man to contact at a well known eastern museum and also the address of a man in the Egyptology department of a major West Coast university. Perhaps one or the other could help them.

Yehneh asked him if, in the future, he would like to accompany them to Egypt. He smiled and said that he had vacation time coming and could perhaps arrange it...Yes, he would like to come.

12

The following week two identical letters were sent, one each to Dr. Y on the East Coast and to Professor Z on the West Coast. Though the letters were similar to the letter sent to Professor X, there were some changes and additions:

...It is with humility, then, that we come to you with this knowledge. We have been told to approach you and have been steered in your direction by Professor X of the Egyptology Department of the University of _____, and we are most willing to lead your archeologists to the designated spot which, with some simple tests, will reveal the substantiality of the pyramid itself.

We need the cooperation of interested parties who have a concession to work in that area, the proper expertise and the appropriate equipment. By equipment, we are speaking at this point about a device similar to the muon projector and/or a machine which will send echoing impulses through strata similar to what oil companies use to explore substrata. We know that a vertical shaft exists, that this type of equipment will register the air pocket(s) and we will have proved our assertion. A muon projector used in this fashion will not be substantially bothered by the electro-magnetic field of the neighboring pyramid.

We will be waiting to hear from you, certain, as we have been told, that the time has come for the world to better understand its history—itself.

Sincerely,

It was not long before Yehneh and Johnstone received replies. The director of the East Coast museum was not in the country at the time. The Associate Curator felt, however, that the museum would "probably not be able to participate."

The reply from Professor Z of the West Coast university was much more encouraging. He informed them that he was "delighted to receive your letter; your project sounds fascinating." He advised them that he did not have proper equipment to explore the area near the Great Pyramid. He suggested they contact the Association for Research and Enlightenment. "I understand," he wrote, "that in the vicinity of the Sphinx, they have carried out research efforts similar to those outlined in your letter."

It was a turning point. From then on Yehneh and Johnstone were to be led in a straight direction, after their somewhat frustrating earlier experiences.

- - - - -

Yehneh asked his guide whether a letter should be sent to the Association for Research and Enlightenment. He was told to do so. Then he asked if it would have been better to send the letter to the Association in the first place. He was told yes.

This confirmed a hunch he had long held. He was to learn over and over in his affairs that asking the right questions of his guide at the right time was all important. Often he would think he had asked the right question only to find later that he should have asked more questions. What answers were possible depended on what questions were asked. Sometimes the plumb line of his inquiry descended only halfway down the well, when in fact it needed to hit bottom.

In this case, though, he was told that the letters needed to go out. It was necessary. The academic and formal researchers had been asked to participate in the initial exploration. Two individuals had been helpful. One had indicated that he personally, at least, would like to accompany them at a future date. This was not a project intended for just occult and mystic researchers. The records were for everyone, concerned everyone, and everyone possible needed to be brought into the fold. All were given their chance.

Yehneh and Johnstone sat down and revised their letter again:

Dear Mr. Cayce:

Mr. Johnstone and I write to you as we have been directed. Separately and with a certain amazement initially, we have been contacted by the guides from the other side of physical consciousness. We have been told, actually reminded, of the location of what will become the most important archeological find in recorded time.

To be specific: buried near the Great Pyramid of Giza is a small preservative pyramid eighteen by twelve feet in dimension. This pyramid was specially constructed to hold the spiritual, philosophical and technical history of the "lost" continents of Lemuria and Atlantis. This gold covered pyramid contains a chamber five feet square in which the information will be found.

It is with humility that we come to you with this knowledge. We have been told to approach you. We are most willing to lead your archeologists to the designated spot which, with some simple tests, will reveal the substantiality of the pyramid itself.

We need the cooperation of interested parties who have a concession to work in that area, the proper expertise and the appropriate equipment. By equipment, we are speaking, at this point, about a device similar to a muon projector and/or a machine which will send echoing impulses through strata similar to what oil companies use to explore substrata. We know that a vertical shaft exists, that this type of equipment will register the air pocket(s) and that then we will have proved our assertion.

Mr. Cayce, there are only two people alive in the world today who know exactly where that pyramid is buried, two of the Seven Fingers of Ra-Ta, who loved their God, their king, their high priest and their people very much and have come back to keep their vow, as it has been written. Those two men were Threegee Sar Tana, an Atlantian immigrant and priest, and Horta Om Innee, "Egyptian" priest and chief engineer, Ra-Ta's most trusted friend. There is a tape-recorded regression of Sar Tana. Professor X of the Department of Egyptology, University of _____, has heard it recently. We would like very much to make it available to you.

We will be waiting to hear from you, certain, as we have been told, that the time has come for the world to better understand its history—itself. We trust this is the letter you have been waiting for.

Sincerely,

13

Thus began Yehneh's and Johnstone's correspondence with the Association for Research and Enlightenment, especially with its Chairman of the Board, Mr. Hugh Lynn Cayce. There was a feeling of exhilaration inside Yehneh. It was as if they had been given a piece to a perplexing puzzle, a piece which had been directly before their eyes but neither had recognized it for what it truly was. Once having grasped it, there was the feeling of "that's it!"

Yehneh was beginning to "see" more and more what he was ready to see, and he realized more each day how we can only see and understand what we have been prepared for, what we have grown into. The domestic house cat does not understand nuclear physics. The selfish man does not understand true charity, otherwise he would practice it. He would be so full of it that he could not help but do so. He would want to.

Both of them waited intently for a response to the letter. It was hard to relax but very necessary to do so. And yet...once understanding the significance of the records, having come to realize the importance of the project, it was extremely difficult not to be excited. Yehneh realized, however, that excitement was not a positive state of mind or body which would contribute to the calm perspicuity that they needed to carry out their mission. And most of all, understanding the importance of the project, they must guard themselves against their egos. Vanity has its myriad forms and varieties, some quick and lush growing, some slow and strangling.

Then, several weeks later, a reply came. Mr. Cayce mentioned how his father had described a cache of records somewhere in front of the Sphinx. He had also indicated a passageway leading from that spot to the right paw of the Sphinx.

He went on to mention some of his efforts in the previous five years to secure permission for research in the area of the Sphinx. Resistivity and acoustical soundings had been made under both the right and left paws, and these soundings had indicated air spaces beneath both. He pointed out how concerned the Egyptians were that no damage be done, and the probe had been limited by certain restrictions as to the depth it could physically penetrate.

What was most encouraging was that he was interested in continuing the research. He was not a man who gave up. He mentioned the problem of funding and offered to meet with them in several weeks when he would be in their vicinity.

That was the kind of reply for which they had been hoping. For awhile, they could relax. It was sweet to anticipate the coming meeting. Everything now seemed to be going straight and true. Or so they thought.

14

Several days later Yehneh and Johnstone replied to Mr. Cayce's letter:

Dear Mr. Cayce:

Mr. Johnstone and I were cheered to receive your letter and to be advised of all that the A.R.E. has been doing to expedite the raising of the records. It will be somewhat difficult, fraught with danger but it is going to happen. We are most anxious to share our information with you.

I am told to tell you that the phrase "in front of the Sphinx" has been somewhat misunderstood. The air pockets your instruments picked up are ritual chambers with a passage that does indeed lead to the shaft wherein lie the records. But this passage is not the "easiest" way to go—because of plugs and politics. Some of the records in the pyramid are in the form of thin manganese tablets—a few fragments in Lemurian, most in Atlan and early "Egyptian" or the language of Khem. The pyramid is relatively light, weighs roughly three thousand pounds, is covered with a light coat of gold and is airtight. Also in the shaft is a crystal and parts of the airship "Volanda." There is much more to say. You can see, sir, our intention is to come straight to the point. We have a lot to say to you but had best wait until we meet. We would prefer at this time that the information in this letter be kept confidential—although E and B should be shown it.

We welcome you to test us in any way you see fit. We are your friends and will do anything in our power to assist you. You may make more inquiries—about who our guides are, who we have been in past lives and why the progression is such as it is.

We look forward to seeing you on the 7th of April. We will be at the conference and would like to get together with you. Perhaps all of you would like to join Mr. Johnstone and myself for dinner. God bless you all.

Love and Light,

P.S. Please send a copy of Mr. Lehner's *The Egyptian Heritage*

15

Yehneh and Johnstone attended the conference on April 7 at the Pick Congress Hotel in Chicago. They listened to the talks given by Gina Cerminara, Elsie Sechrist and Harmon Bro, coming alway from them convinced more than ever that the Association for Research and Enlightenment was fulfilling a large and growing need in the spiritual development of those who were interested and would listen.

Late in the afternoon they met Mr. Hugh Lynn Cayce in his hotel room and discussed their previous correspondence. Mr. Cayce was quite friendly and recapitulated for them the effort that the A.R.E. had made in the vicinity of the

Sphinx and reaffirmed his commitment to keep working in the area if more funding could be found.

Yehneh and his friend offered to point out the exact spot under which the archives were buried, as representatives of the White Brotherhood, Order of Melchizedek, provided that Mr. Cayce himself accompany them there. Mr. Cayce suggested it might be just as easy to tell him the location and he could have it checked out or, alternatively, for them to make the trip to Giza and point out the spot to Mr. Mark Lehner, who was one of the A.R.E.'s representatives in the area. He promised that the A.R.E. would give full credit where due to the Brotherhood.

This did not satisfy Yehneh and Johnstone. They pointed out that it was part of their vows to make the trip and to indicate the spot to him in person. At this point they mentioned their own funding problems. They asked if the A.R.E. would be willing to pay their expenses for such a trip.

Mr. Cayce maintained that the fund from which money for the project had come in the past was depleted. There simply was not enough money at that time to pay for such a trip. He promised to send them some information about low-cost group rates obtained through one of the travel agencies. Then he suggested that if the information they brought back from such a trip proved to be accurate, he could probably raise more money for research and would gladly reimburse them.

They talked about a convenient future date at which time all three of them might travel together to Giza and the pyramids. It was an amiable meeting all right, undermined by financial consid-erations which soon, unknown to all of them, would threaten the entire project.

16

Several days past, and then Yehneh and his friend wrote another letter:

Dear Mr. Cayce:

Congratulations on the successful program at the Pick Congress. Mr. Johnstone and I were very pleased to get to meet you personally, and E and B as well.

Financial success has come to the A.R.E. and especially at this time, as it is intended to—so that we can get on with the work of raising the records. Your father said that it would be "those that are the initiates" who would appear at the right moment—if it were God's will. For it to be God's will, we must all work together as selflessly as possible, forgetting personal glory as we realize how important to mankind's future the dissemination of the information in the records is.

It will be made clear that these are the records of the White Brotherhood, why there is a Brotherhood, why Ra-Ta returned, why his son is fulfilling his vow as perpetuator of the knowledge and builder of a custodial organization that could offer financial support for the actual raising of the records and later support for the dissemination of the information in the records. This great "son" has lighted the night with his loyalty and unswearving endeavor. He must not forget that he, too, is a Brother.

We all will get our just reward but we must work together, honestly, enthusiastically, and with love and faith.

Yours truly

- - - - -

At this time a great mistake was made. At a later time, rereading the correspondence of those days, Yehneh would become ashamed. There was something wrong with the tone of voice of those letters. There was a presumptuousness on Yehneh's and Johnstone's part that showed between the words. Often what is not said but implied is more important than what is said. Vanity, like a creeping vine, had begun to strangle the humility that was necessary for such a project to succeed.

Johnstone came to Yehneh with a list of items that he said should be included in a written agreement that should accompany, should be attached to a letter:

AGREEMENT

It is agreed that Yehneh and Mr. Johnstone, members of the White Brotherhood and representatives of the Order of Melchizedek, will indicate to the Association for Research and Enlightenment and its associates, to the best of their ability, in the presence of

Hugh Lynn Cayce, the location of the shaft wherein lie the ancient records of the Brotherhood: that the aforesaid will render every reasonable assistance to expedite the raising of the records; that the aforesaid will offer help translating said records; that the aforesaid will offer their services where reasonable in publicizing the importance of said records; that the aforesaid acknowledge the great debt owed to the A.R.E. and Mr. Hugh Lynn Cayce for supplying the physical wherewithal and much of the inspiration for getting the job done...

There was more. Yehneh and Johnstone asked for six thousand dollars apiece and round trip air fare as well as a meal allowance. Upon recovery of the records, they were to receive a bonus of twenty-five thousand dollars apiece. There was also mention of offering their services for future expeditions in search of Essene records in the vicinity of Khirbat Qumran. For this also, they had a price.

Yehneh did not like the idea. He argued that it was the work of the

Brotherhood and that one did not ask for money in return for being of service to one's brothers. His friend argued that it was not reasonable to expect them to undertake a trip, perhaps several months long, without compensation for the salary loses. They had families to care for. He felt they did not have the money themselves and that the Brotherhood would provide through the agency of the Association for Research and Enlightenment, whose founder had just such projects in mind years ago when he began his organization. Was he not, after all, Ra-Ta? Didn't he even now in spirit want the records raised as much as them, the same records he himself had helped collect and put away in safe keeping?

Johnstone insisted he had received the articles of the Agreement directly from the Brotherhood and his own guides.

Yehneh yielded to these arguments. Why didn't he refuse to coauthor such a document? The question would come to nag at his soul for months and years later. If he was in communication with his guide, why hadn't he heard clearly when he asked advice from him. Why hadn't he given a firm "No, not that way" response to Johnstone?

Looking back, Yehneh tried to understand what had happened. His guide continually advised him about the need for humility. His guide finally told him and his friend as well that they both needed to learn more humility.

Yehneh *had* asked his guide at the time and he thought he heard correctly. Perhaps he had heard what he wanted to hear. It was so easy to do. One could lower one's guard for just a second, and vanity and half of Pandora's box would be there whispering in one's ear whatever one wanted to hear or what one was willing to hear. Everything from elementals, elementaries or one's selfish self could clamor for attention. How often we hear what we want to hear, he was reminded, see what we want to see regardless of the greater reality.

Later he knew his friend had heard what he had wanted to hear, in fact was still doing so. Yehneh was to learn how important it is to keep one's life spiritually, mentally and emotionally under control at all times. And that, as almost every man knows, is not always easy on this plane of existence. But it is necessary. It must be accomplished. The higher one reaches into the knowledge of the Masters, the more it becomes necessary for a man to keep his life controlled so that it does not interfere with the work delegated to him by the Elder Brothers.

It really didn't matter whether it was Yehneh or Johnstone who first came up with the idea of the special Agreement. They both endorsed the idea because they were not ready spiritually, mentally and emotionally to do what they sought to do. They had a lot to learn.

Today Yehneh is more aware of the narrowness and difficulty of the path he chose. He realizes how hard and treacherous "the slings and arrows of outrageous fortune" can be. He hopes that by relating these events, that others will see them as examples of how we are all here, on this physical plane, to learn to understand the physical life better, to learn to marshal our emotions and mind in a direction that leads to the growth and compassionate control of the spiritual nature. And to learn that very little happens accidentally. We are the authors of our own good fortune, and through the Law of Consequence (rebirth and karma), we come slowly to recognize our responsibility for the directions, both positive and negative, that our growth takes.

The spirit which precedes all, and succeeds all, and is a part of the eternal abiding Creator, does not know selfishness, loves all equally and is willing to give itself freely to whomsoever would commune with it.

17

Mr. Cayce replied shortly. He reiterated his earlier statement at the Pick Congress that he did not have sufficient funds at the moment in the Sphinx project account to cover the expenses of such a venture as they were proposing. He repeated his offer to reimburse them if they would fund themselves initially and come up with something that could be checked.

He went on to mention the A.R.E.'s efforts in more detail, how it had dug a sand mound across the road from the Sphinx and located an ancient tomb going back to the time of Kufu. This he pointed out was just another of the innumerable tombs in the Giza complex. He also pointed out to them how many psychic "sensitives" had reconfirmed for him over the years the accuracy of the material his father, Edgar Cayce, had given about a passageway and chambers below both the right and left paws of the Sphinx. He indicated, and rightfully so, that this was important progress, work which he hoped would lead to the record chambers.

Many sensitives had suggested to him places to dig. He pointed out further the difficulty of sorting the wheat from the chaff. The A.R.E. could not dig everywhere. What if they were in his position? he asked. How would you sort these things out?

Then he proposed to them a question, actually two questions, which dealt with his relationship with his father. If they could answer these questions, it would be a proof to him that they had accurate information or were, in fact, in actual communication with his father. If they could answer these two questions, he would reevaluate his position as it then stood.

Mr. Cayce said he planned to fly to Egypt in May. Would they like to meet him there at their own expense? He would undertake to check out what they found there. He said he believed they were sincere in what they had received but knew well how difficult physical research could be. He ended his letter by saying he had liked them upon meeting them and hoped that their information was true. Truth, as the poet said, would hopefully will out.

18

It was a fair and friendly letter. How could Mr. Cayce, after all, be sure they were representing the Brotherhood? And, essentially, who were "they"? They were human beings, vulnerable to all the failings humans are heir to. They were not perfected in their parts, surely not. Perhaps not as much as they needed to be.

Yehneh was all too aware of his position and yet partially blinded. Who would believe the great negative energy that was amassed against them? How do you explain such things to people who do not understand these negative forces? How do you explain the telephone call in the middle of the night, for instance, speaking of the great cloud of negative energy hovering over his house and the voice that said, "Why, you don't even know who you are," and the turning away and even death of some who had vowed to aid in the great project of raising the records. For Yehneh knew even then how much cooperation was needed among all parties involved for the records to ever come out into the light of day. And for that kind of cooperation to be possible, men's attitudes must change, including Johnstone's and his own.

The records of Thoth are the history of the "ancient" world, more ancient than most historians have dared to think. They tell of civilizations much more advanced than most of us have consciously suspected—or been taught. The Great Pyramid of Giza was raised to the glory of God, the Creator. It is not, as so many think, simply a burial tomb. And its construction is ascribed popularly to a pharaoh who, in fact, had nothing to do with building it. It does, however, proclaim "He who is to come," the turning of the life wave and the beginning of a different world order from the one to which we have all become too accustomed.

The records of Thoth (Thoth himself was an earlier Melchizedek spirit; that is, one who is impregnated directly with the Logos, the Word, God the Father, as was Jesus) are direct links between "ancient" time, the present time, and the imminent future moment, which is very close at hand, when "He who is to come," the Christ, will return to direct the new world order.

Jesus who became the Christ ushered in the present time. He links the ancient with the future time when He will come to rule over this new order. The records of Thoth indicate the progression. Man will be able to see from the records the great continuity of the Coming. Men have not in the past seen clearly this continuity—how advanced civilizations existed earlier in time than most archeologists have been willing to admit—because they have continually maintained there is a lack of evidence.

The records are the most convinving evidence to even the most "scientifically" demanding mind. Much of the recurring woefulness of this cycle of humanity has been due to a lack of understanding of man's true past. The records will make it possible for man to know himself better. The knowledge will be there, is there now. He must be willing to search and to see. He must have the will. He must seek. "Seek and ye shall find. Ask and ye shall be given." Yes. Given enlightenment with which to see clearly, truly. How accurate those words of the Master are today, as always.

"He who is to come" is the Christ. And who is the Christ? The man (Son of Man) known as Jesus developed more rapidly, perfected himself more quickly, than the rest of mankind both in other realms and in His earth lives. He was outstanding as a developing entity in the early history of the planet (as, for instance, when Amelius), and in later lives he demonstrated a growth toward perfection which made him a leader among men, as, for example, Enoch, Joshua, Joseph, Ikhnaton and Jesus. He was so outstanding that he found great favor with the Elder Brothers and the Creator and Sustainer of all things.

He was sent on a mission to earth to

qualify Himself to lead His fellow men back to the path brightened by His Father's Light and away from the negative teaching and influence of entities which had rebelled against the order of the Creator's original creation. This creation and ordering was delegated in its detail to His subordinate creative agents working through Him, the Elohim (Hebrew plural of ''gods'') led by leaders such as Jehovah. Some of these agents, rebellious ones, lost their sense of humility and challenged the ordained leadership. By so doing, they challenged the Creator's laws and the Creator Himself.

Before man can become inheritor of eternal life (symbolized as the Tree of Life) and be given the understanding of cosmic powers, which is part of that inheritance, before he can be entrusted with that immense knowledge, he must develop within himself a true knowledge of positive and negative cosmic forces. He must learn to use this knowledge with total responsibility. The rebellious ones among the Elohim demonstrated the dangers of a spirit losing its spiritual balance.

Man chose to know. He chose the knowledge of the Tree of Positive (Good) and Negative (Evil). He desired to know it all and at once. He became "initiated" into both the positive and the negative (good and evil). But he soon found that the negative, the great cosmic contrapuntal rhythm which exists in the Creator at His sufferance, has a way of turning man away from the Creator's Light or Cosmic Knowledge. To know the negative is often to become tainted with it. It is all too easy to begin to mirror that which one says he abhors or thinks he is strong enough to resist. As man began exploring the negative, he became blinded and confused. And he "forgot" far too much that he needed to know; he also began to break the covenants he made with the Elohim and the Creator.

The man Jesus, the most advanced spiritually of all men up to that time, came back to qualify Himself to lead His fellow men, once they took the initiative themselves, each one separately by an act of seeking cosmic truth, into a New Age on this plane of existence. By facing the most extreme assaults of the negative and relying on the Creator's Light, he did qualify. He did not, when challenged after forty foodless days, turn stone into bread for self's sake. He did not throw Himself down to His physical death from the heights of the Temple and call upon His Creator to perform a "miracle" to save Him. He refused a false kingship of mere physicality and selfish, personal power. He qualified because He had overcome all selfish regard. He became a responsible conduit for the Creator's trust, just as every man has it within him to become so. He knew the cosmic laws that made seeming "miracles" but refused to use these laws for His own self-interest. It is a law of the Brotherhoods that this knowledge be used for the benefit of others, never for self.

Many of those who do insist on breaking this law have turned from their Creator in a frenzy of selfishness that knows no limit. Like a spark that has been too long away from the Divine Fire, their energy diminishes in proportion to the time away. They can only energize themselves by feeding on the psychic energy of their victims.

When John the Baptist submerged the man Jesus (Son of Man), the Melchizedek spirit (the Word) entered directly into Him. He became at that moment, Jesus the Christ (Son of God). What this really means is that He came into a state of total harmony with the Creator's laws and will.

Yehneh came to understand this. As his eyes became more opened, he began to see more clearly, and he began to realize that he saw more clearly as an act of will, and more clearly still as an act of faith. He was seeking truth. He came to see, through his guide, the Master of Masters, that we are all Sons of Man. That is our evolutionary heritage.

But there is a much greater heritage that must be claimed. We are all sparks from the Creator's Light. We each have within us a part of our Creator's Spirit. And in most of us it is asleep most of the time. We are all, in short, Sons of God—if we will earn our heritage by right thought and action and claim it.

Christ said, and the Masters and those knowledgeable know how true it is, that "If ye have faith as a grain of mustard seed, ye shall say unto this mountain, remove hence to younder place; and it shall remove; and nothing shall be impossible unto you." He also said, "Verily, verily, I say unto you, He that believeth in me, the works that I do shall he do also; and greater works than these shall he do; because I go unto my Father."

Yehneh came to realize how few people understood what that means. Nothing is impossible. "He who is to come" is surely the Christ. And after Christ, it is you. You. You are the enlightened one of the future. The Buddhists have a name for that one, Maitreya—the enlightened one to come.

Christ is saying we are His equals with the Creator if we claim our heritage. To give man eternal life with such powers before he learned how to responsibly use them was not the Creator's wish. That would have caused negative consequences to be sure. The Creator's plan for man is to have him develop the way of Jesus along the positive path until he can become a responsible creator in his own right.

Jesus the man is the great example for mankind in this world. He has shown us how we can develop spiritually. He has blazed a trail of Light. He is our Elder Brother. Let us recognize the best example to emulate and emulate Him. He has proved to us what can be done and shown us what must be done.

To understand the Master Jesus who became the Christ in this way is to inherit a living brother and teacher. It is to love Him even more for His accomplishment, for His selflessness, for His love. One must realize that even Christ, and other advanced spirits and teachers such as Buddha and Mohammed, lived many lives learning to understand creation on this plane of existence. They did not perfect themselves overnight or in a few years. They did, however, learn a bit faster than most of us. One suspects that they kept their minds and spirits open a bit more than most of us. They sought harder, longer with more patience. They desired the truth a little more than us. And they grew in spirit, consequently, at a greater pace.

- - - - -

The reply to Mr. Cayce's two questions was mailed. Yehneh and Johnstone were about to get a lesson in humility. The return letter left them stunned and doubting themselves. At first their inclination was to wonder if he was not playing games with them. Could it be that he did not want them around?

Mr. Cayce informed them that their information was not accurate. They had missed the truth completely. He hoped that they would check their results and try to find out just exactly why they were so far from the mark. Sometimes, he added, we learn more from checking than from any other way.

This began many months of inquiry, months in which Yehneh felt little progress was being made to bring the project to fruition. He and Johnstone seemed to be taking two steps backward for each step forward. And the tension between them grew.

19

Yehneh awoke one morning and began hobbling about. His left leg was very sore and the soreness extended upward into his lower back, as if the kundalini had been attacked. He had strong feelings that something was seriously wrong. It wasn't the first time of late that he had those feelings. They had been coming with increasing frequency.

He told his friend when he talked to him again that he was greatly disturbed and that his back seemed to be injured. Johnstone said that Yehneh had been rescued by the Elder Brothers and certain other advanced entities from associating with negative entities on the astral plane. Yehneh wanted consciously to deny this.

He did not like admitting to actions which seemed so contrary to what he believed in and which were so at odds with what he was trying to accomplish.

Johnstone suggested Yehneh have a serious talk with his guide. This made him uneasy. He felt his friend was, for some reason, trying to make him feel guilty. For several days Yehneh did try to talk with his guide. He would think he had done so. Yet Johnstone would tell him to try again. Johnstone was sure he, Yehneh, was not talking to his guide.

Then who was he talking to? Yehneh prayed to God to give him strength. He prayed that negative entities and forces be forced back from him. He wanted to talk to his guide clearly and to have that confident, relaxed feeling within himself that he had successfully done so.

Finally, the truth rose into his consciousness. He allowed it to after several days of resistance. What his guide told him shamed him. At first he did not understand how he could have done such a thing. With further questioning of his guide, and after meditating, he began to understand, he thought, what his motives had been. And he saw how wrong his motives had been.

He had been approached and offered help by certain powerful negative entities. They would help him and his friend raise the records. They could be, they assured him, of inestimable aid. If they withdrew their opposition to such a venture, and actually reversed their position, it would not be long at all before the records surfaced. There was, of course, one large condition. Yehneh, and Johnstone as well, would have to be willing to work with them in the future. How much did he want the records to surface for the good of mankind, anyway? He could talk his friend into such a deal, couldn't he? Well, couldn't he?

Yehneh had always said to himself that he would be willing to sacrifice himself to see the records brought to the light of day. Here was his chance. He was on the razor's edge of forsaking his vows as a Brother and consummating the agreement with the promise that he would try to bring Johnstone along as well, when positive spirit entities came to his rescue. He was then struck on the astral plane in the kundalini in the struggle to free himself.

When Yehneh told his friend all this, Johnstone was not surprised. It was what he already knew. Yehneh apologized to him and asked his forgiveness. He had, he admitted, no right to bargain away another's soul. Hardly. It just proved how confused and misdirected his thinking on the subconscious level had become lately. It also indicated how far out of synchrony his consciousness was with his subconscious. This was definitely not the way to sacrifice oneself or one's friends. He hoped now he had learned better. Johnstone said he forgave him, and he felt much relieved.

He then prayed to God for forgiveness. He asked the positive spirit entities who had aided him for forgiveness. And then he prayed that the project might continue and, God and the Brotherhood willing, that he might be allowed to participate.

20

That was not the end of it. Yehneh still had not learned that one must have no conscious or unconscious association whatsoever with these negative entities for any reason on this plane, the astral plane or any other plane. And he was to learn why. It almost cost him his soul-life and put in danger the eternal spark of the Creator that abides within it.

One morning he awoke after a particularly bad "dream." He had dreamed that he must go to Turner's square. He was to attend a meeting there.

He was certain he was to go but he didn't like the feeling this gave him. Something once again was wrong, very wrong. He called Johnstone and told him he needed his help. He told him the story, admitting that he was too nervous to trust the answers he was getting. Johnstone sighed. He told Yehneh to continue to try to reach his guide. He could not help him. No, he could not help him. His own guide had told him as much. It was between Yehneh, his guide and the Creator.

This answer depressed Yehneh. Somehow for a moment he felt let down. He was looking for something, someone to blame for the pressure inside of him. He began to wonder if he was a Judas, come to betray the Creator, his guide, his Brothers, his friends and himself. Never, since first breaking through to his guide and learning consciously about his vows concerning the Egyptian project, had he felt so depressed. He didn't know consciously what he had done and yet he felt desperate.

He prayed. He asked God to help him. He prayed that he hear his guide clearly. There was, he could feel, tremendous negative energy interfering with that communication. Yet he knew that if his head were in more perfect balance, he would not be having the trouble he was having communicating. All the negative energy in the cosmos cannot stop an entity from communicating with the Creator and his own guide if God so desires or if the Light of the Creator continues to burn brightly within the entity so that contact is never broken.

Finally, he felt that he was, indeed, speaking directly to his guide. He asked him to pray for him to God, to ask the Creator's help in guiding him. Then he asked his guide if he must surely go to Turner's square. He was told that he had given his word and must go. He asked if it were dangerous to his spirit. He was told, yes, his spirit was in great danger.

For several days he did nothing. Then he spoke to his guide again. He asked him if it were not about time that we went to Turner's square. His guide said that it was time. He asked his guide what he must do. What would the Creator have him do? His guide told him to go to Turner's square and to recite the Lord's Prayer. He was to continue to recite it no matter what. That was it.

Yehneh would try to follow instructions this time. No matter what. He went off to prepare himself, musing over in his mind how far afield he had come in his wish to serve God and his Brothers in the Egyptian project with honor. He felt that he had dishonored himself before all that was most holy in his life. He felt like a pariah.

21

In the calm of the late evening hours he put himself into a deep trance and projected himself to Turner's square. Consciously he did not know the way. Subconsciously he went right to the spot.

Suddenly he was standing on a raised block, a square. Seated before him and above him was a powerful negative entity. He began to pray, to recite the Lord's Prayer as he had been instructed. This angered the entity greatly. There is a cosmic fury, to be sure, and Yehneh witnessed a display of it.

He was given a lecture. He was told that the primary principle of the cosmos was division and disintegration, and that the Creator cared not otherwise. Nothingness. Everything was assigned, swallowed up ultimately into primordial nothingness. Division. Obliteration. Death. An endless cycle of destruction.

The entity was truly furious. The Lord's Prayer was hateful to him. He shouted to Yehneh that he could not do this. He beckoned to his aides, and Yehneh was brought farther forward, his head was lowered and then it was severed from his body. Cut off cleanly, instantaneously. He watched as if from a distance as his head came off and rolled to the side.

Then something wonderful happened. His head came back, floated in the air back to his body, and he was in one piece again. Yehneh realized that for a moment in cosmic time he had been dead. His astral head had been severed from his astral body. On the earth plane he never would have come out of his trance. He would have been found physically dead as well.

Then it happened. He heard the Creator's voice. It was truly the Word. It said, "Let nothing put asunder that which I have made whole again."

And in another cosmic instant Yehneh was back on the earth plane still reciting, over and over again, the Lord's Prayer. He prayed then in thankfulness to God and asked forgiveness.

- - - - -

By questioning his guide, Yehneh began to understand what had been happening. He was told that on the earth plane one should go out of one's way to make friends with those individuals who have been one's enemies. For that matter, one should befriend all men at all times regardless.

On the astral plane, this is not necessarily true. One must avoid contact with negative entities there at all times. To take notice of them is to give them energy. It is not the Creator's wish that these entities which are in rebellion against His Order should be given attention. They should, must be ignored.

Yehneh had known many of these

entities before the world as we know it now ever existed. They had appealed to him as old friends. Even though they were out of favor with the Creator, they appealed to Yehneh to let them help him. At least let them speak with him. Hadn't they been friends? Would he turn away so easily from those he had known?

His guide reiterated the necessity of turning away. Yehneh could not expect to survive encounters with these displaced entities on his own. Their negative energy was great and, as he had proved, he was quite capable of being duped. He had also duped himself. After all, good old friends don't try to enslave you or sever the life-force from you. That was common sense.

Somehow he had developed at least two very poor ideas. One was that nothing mattered so long as the records were brought to the light of day. The other was his egocentric idea of self-sacrifice.

He had to learn that neither God nor the Brotherhood would support the kind of actions he had been indulging in. How the records were brought out mattered very much. For them to ever see the light of day, entities such as himself must be in spiritual harmony and must have their inner natures, their conscious and subconscious selves, in balance with God's will.

Yehneh must also get over his false idea of giving his life away. There was only one way to give one's life and he had not yet found it. He must look into himself, plumb his depths honestly and fearlessly, to understand where he had failed. He must strive for a humility that had always come very hard for him. Then perhaps he might see and know the greater truth.

And he must learn that he was responsible for what he did on the astral plane. That was why harmony between the conscious and subconscious was so important. Because the left hand did not know what the right hand was doing was no excuse. The danger was always present that the entity would become uncoordinated. That was one of the main reasons why Masters, who had already learned their own lessons about the physical plane, hesitated to reincarnate even though they desired to serve their fellow humans. It was difficult enough breaking through to find out the meaning of one's mission on this plane. The chances of getting out of harmony were great. Yet a man was responsible for his actions if he did so.

It was possible, under pressure from the negative or by one's own missteps, to fall into retrogressive behavior. Yet even with all these dangers, many Masters had reincarnated at this point in history. More so than at any one time before. That spoke strongly for their selflessness and great love for humanity. It was their desire to be present and available to help at the moment of the great change of the life wave into a new spiritual dimension of life.

22

The days and months went by. Yehneh felt that he had failed. He had not given up completely on the project, but there seemed most of the time little prospect that he would be a part of any future attempts to raise the records. If by chance he were a part of future attempts, the prospect seemed to be associated with a distant time. He had to grow some first. He knew that. Sometimes a hopeless feeling began to sweep through him like a cold wind and chilled his soul to the core.

Johnstone had withdrawn into himself. He seemed to have lost all interest in the project. He spoke of other things, seldom of the records and then only after Yehneh brought them up.

Yehneh couldn't quite decide whether he had disappointed his friend, and his friend had decided for himself that the project was off, or whether his friend thought that Yehneh was no longer a part of it and therefore did not wish to discuss it with him. Certainly he did not seem interested. He spoke of domestic troubles and negative entities trying to gain power over his family and himself.

Now they spoke very seldom to one another. When they did, Johnstone seemed obsessed with his struggle with these negative entities. Yehneh offered to talk about them but he was elusive. He did not want to talk. Yehneh thought he could understand what his friend was going through. He knew such feelings well enough. What disturbed him, though, was his friend's insistence that he was in control of everything. He would, he said, defeat his adversaries. He spoke of gaining power over them.

This kind of talk worried Yehneh. It seemed like he and Johnstone were getting nowhere. They were retrogressing, and the pyramid project was receding with the speed of light years in the opposite direction away from them.

Mr. Cayce was silent. There were no more letters. Hardly a day went by that he did not think of the records. He knew that if God willed the records out, they would come out. And he yearned still to be a partner in such a great venture.

23

Months had passed. Nothing happened. Mr. Cayce remained silent. The drought passing over the United States seemed as spiritual as much as physical, and internally Yehneh felt as if his soul had been seared. He felt as if his soul were withering, drying up into a static husk of its former self. He felt in need of healing.

Time continued to pass very slowly for him. Then one day during the coldest part of the next winter, Yehneh's wife turned to him and said, "You know, I think you should go to Egypt. Somehow I feel you're supposed to go very soon."

Yehneh said, "You know, I don't know why, but I think you're right. I'll ask the Master."

He had got into the habit of calling his guide, "Master." In the beginning he had called him Hotep and for quite a while afterward. Then he had asked if he would prefer to be called something else. Would Christ be preferable? He had been told that "Master" would be best, and from that moment on he called his guide simply "Master."

Earlier he had asked the Master if the Brotherhood wanted him to continue working on the raising of the records. Was he still, after all, a part of the project?

The Master had told him he was still part of the project. Yehneh didn't have the courage then to ask more questions at that time. Things had settled into what seemed like a static pattern. Perhaps there was new growth beneath the snow, but to Yehneh it seemed like a spiritual winter. He was no longer so sure of himself.

He calmed himself and asked the Master that large question. The answer thrilled him. Yes, he should prepare to travel to Egypt. The time had come for him to take a trip. He began to realize how great the love is and how profound the willingness of the Creator to forgive. He came to realize that we are given every chance to see the Light, provided that we love Him and are seeking Him. Then we may stumble and He will pull us up. The secret writing of our heart's desire is an open book to Him.

Something made Yehneh know that the appropriate time for the trip was the latter part of December. He just knew it. For some reason it was necessary to begin the trip in the old year before the new year began. He asked the Master, who confirmed for him his inner suspicions.

He was told that the twenty-ninth or shortly after was appropriate. It would indeed be best if he began the trip before the first of January. He now had no doubt as to the reality of what was happening. It seemed as if it had its own inevitability. It was going to happen now. If there were tears in his eyes, they signified neither fear nor hope but gratefulness for his opportunity.

His wife dreamed vividly that all those directly involved with the project met together in the Desire World on the astral plane. When she awoke the next morning she remembered the "dream" and related it to him. It seemed to verify something Johnstone had once said about a necessary meeting with the Elder Brothers before any trip was possible. Sure enough, the inevitability of things in their right order proclaimed itself. The Master verified for him the necessity of a meeting that he had little conscious memory of—except through his soul mate, which is, after all, himself.

24

He asked the Master in his excitement if he shouldn't be doing something, if there was perhaps something he was forgetting. Previously when he had sounded out the Master as to the advisability of further action, he had been told to wait. That had put him in the doldrums.

Now he was told to act. He was to send a letter to Mr. Cayce before he did anything else.

Yehneh's spirit began to soar like a hawk released from the wrist guard. It took so little now to make hope take flight within him. He wanted to make amends for his former foolishness. He wanted to serve God and the Master and the

Brotherhood in any way he could. He knew the necessity of keeping emotional balance, and in the mood he was in, he almost feared he might not.

He sat down eagerly and wrote the Chairman of the A.R.E.

Dear Mr. Cayce,

I am willing to meet with you and your staff to be regressed under controlled conditions in regard to the buried records pyramid of the Great Pyramid. I will go into trance for this. You might wish to have a hypnotist knowledgeable in these matters present. I believe you will find this procedure productive of the truth that concerns us all.

I teach and am tied up with related duties until Thanksgiving time. If it is convenient for you, I can be in Virginia Beach around that time. If all goes well, we might be in Egypt in January.

You may ask me any questions you wish except to state the exact location of the records, which I can not do until we are standing on the spot and I have been given permission to do so.

As for any other conditions, there are none. I will pay my own travel expenses to Virginia Beach and beyond. I hope we are understood on that point. A mistake was made. I apologize.

Professor X of the University of _____ has indicated earlier that he might be interested in such a trip. It would be fitting to have him along in January if he's still willing.

I will be awaiting word from you.

> Light and Love
> White Brotherhood
> Order of Melchizedek

25

And then Yehneh had to wait. He waited for the reply, trying to maintain a composure that he knew was essential for success if he were to participate in the raising of the records.

All his life, he had been too impulsive, too fast off the starting block. He had been too often the emotional hare when life called for the reasonable tortoise.

It was only a matter of weeks but it did seem like longer. No reply came. Then finally a letter.

Yehneh was informed by Mr. Cayce's personal secretary that Mr. Cayce was out of town for the rest of November. He would see the letter upon his return in

December. Perhaps, it was stated, something could be arranged over the Christmas holiday season, when Mr. Cayce was expected to be in town.

Yehneh spoke with the Master. What should he do? He could hardly pretend that he wasn't somewhat disappointed by this state of affairs.

The Master told him to continue to prepare for a trip to Egypt during the latter part of December. He asked if he should talk to Johnstone, perhaps query his thoughts about such a trip. He was told to speak with his friend but to do so carefully.

- - - - -

When Yehneh met with Johnstone he felt that he was uncomfortable but trying very hard to hide this from him. His friend still spoke of negative forces trying to overpower him. Yehneh suggested he ignore them, that it was necessary to do so.

"Let it go," he said. "It's not really that important to gain the upper hand as such. There are more important things. Ask God to exorcise these things from around you."

But he could see that his friend was not hearing him. He was caught up in his own personal drama and insisted he could handle it all himself, which was a grave mistake.

"What about the pyramid project?"

Johnstone said that he had not thought about the records in months. He added rather mysteriously that there were some other things which needed to be taken care of first.

Yehneh said he didn't think there was much more important now than the records. It was their vow to work toward their recovery.

He felt Johnstone was not hearing him at all. He had had his attention diverted and only he could bring himself back. His friend looked right at him but did not hear him. Yehneh asked him if he were talking to his guide. He indicated that he had other guides, other voices now feeding him information.

This worried Yehneh greatly. He had been told by the Master that his friend was diverted but to hear him say it, to hear him dismiss the project as unimportant at this time greatly affected him. He shook Johnstone's hand, and they parted—for the time to walk their separate paths.

26

Yehneh asked the Master what to do about his friend. He was becoming more and more worried about him. The Master said to show him affection and help him when he sought help. Otherwise, Johnstone must see the light first himself before others could, or he would let them, discuss his situation meaningfully with them.

Yehneh knew the path well enough to know that one walked it alone, and often painfully, for some time before one came to realize how many helpful fellow travelers were also walking lovingly beside him. Then they began to appear in the light, as out of a mist, offering aid to those who need it. Yehneh knew that his friend knew this. But his friend had now forgot.

The loving figures of light about his friend were receding into the mist again. Johnstone must remember them again. Until then, Yehneh must be cautious about what he said to him.

Yehneh asked the Master if the project would continue without his friend's active participation, and he was told it would. Weren't the both of them to have continued together? The Master answered affirmatively. Yehneh then asked if the Master still wanted him to take the trip to Egypt. He was told to continue to make plans, that later, hopefully, his friend would rejoin those working actively on the project.

These words both elated and disappointed Yehneh. The project, after all, was to continue but he had lost his best friend along the way, at least for the time being, this great friend he had known in so many lives. He hoped they would soon be working effectively together again, and he knew that no matter the power of the negative energy that was brought against the project, if the Creator and the Brotherhood wanted the records to see the light of day, they would see the light of day. That was as certain as the rising of the sun.

27

Soon Yehneh began to react almost automatically. He got out an almanac and an ephemeris and certain things became more clear.

On December 29, 1980 there would be a conjunction between Jupiter and the moon and one between Saturn and the moon, followed by an actual conjunction between Jupiter and Saturn on December 31. All this served cosmically as a sort of triggering device for a pattern of energetic phenomena to follow the next year and far into and beyond the next decade. The moon would be on the equator December 29 and at apogee the next day.

Thus began a revealing cosmic pattern that was intimately connected with the Egyptian project and Yehneh's own horoscope. Within the first week of January, 1981 there would be six conjunctions, following the Jupiter-Saturn conjunction of December 31. Actually seven planets would conjunct in a period of seven days, spanning the two years. The Earth would reach perihelion, its point closest to the sun, on the first of the month. On the sixth would come a new moon.

As Yehneh began to study the stars and question the Master, he understood much more—what was happening astronomically and astrologically which was of so much significance to everyone alive today. He began to see that these line-ups, these conjunctions, and those of the summer later in the new year, were signaling the Great Line-Up that would be taking place in 1982 when the visible planets of the solar system would be virtually in line. This was similar to the equally significant line-up shortly after the turn of the century.

Yehneh soon learned that these line-ups presaged the great physical changes about to overtake the earth. It was a time of great physical and spiritual change on the earth plane that could be compared to a cleansing process. The direction of the life wave was about to change. Those who would physically survive and adapt best were those who were most spiritually ready for the transformation. Much of the knowledge in the records of Thoth would help people understand their history and, therefore, themselves better. It would, in brief, help them become more spiritually ready—if they were willing to be so.

Yehneh's own horoscope was intimately related to the last week in December of the old year and the first week in January of the new year. It was a time most favorable for the kind of journey he was to undertake.

Yehneh was born in May under the sign of Taurus with a Libra rising in his first house. His ruling planet was Venus and Neptune appeared in his twelfth house.

When Yehneh looked at the series of conjunctions, they began to make sense to him. On the first, when the Earth would be closest to the sun, Yehneh, son of his

Father, would be closest, as would the plane of existence upon which he dwelt and in which he was working, to the chief symbol and source of the Creator's Light in this cosmic system. The next day Uranus would be in conjunction with the moon, suggesting a time of metamorphosis. On the fourth would occur a conjunction between Venus and the moon and another between Neptune and the moon.

These two planets, so intimately related to the rhythms of Yehneh's life, would conjunct themselves on the next day, the fifth, which Christians know as Twelfth Night. The sixth would bring a conjunction between Mercury and the moon, the Epiphany, and a new moon as well. With the conjunction between Mars and the moon on the seventh, with its release of energy, the immediate cycle for Yehneh would end.

He saw the great significance of the conjunction between Jupiter and Saturn. Throughout history these conjunctions had marked important turning points in the affairs of life on earth, and especially pertinent to spiritual development when happening near to or in Libra or the other two air signs of the Zodiac, Aquarius and Gemini. Those happening in Libra itself were technically called mutation conjunctions. The conjunction of Jupiter and Saturn that would occur on December 31, 1980 would be followed in rapid succession by a Jupiter-Saturn conjunction in Libra in the summer of 1981.

Yehneh saw all this as signaling generally not only the ending of the old year and the beginning of the new, but a definite cosmic indication of the great changes to come not only to himself but to all men.

On the first of January he would be drawn close to the symbolic Creator, the Sun, whose Light bathes the world and brings life to all that is living. Then would come the indicator of change, the conjunction between Uranus and the moon. On the third his ruling planet, Venus, and also Neptune would be in conjunction with the moon but not with each other until the next day. That suggested to him an extremely important moment.

If he were going to Egypt to keep his vow to return to help raise the records, this would be the key moment. Neptune in his twelfth house indicated the psychic gift the Creator of all had endowed him with. At the moment of conjunction between his ruling planet and Neptune, he should, perhaps, God willing, see and remember most clearly.

He prayed to God that whatever might happen, it would please Him and the Master and his Brothers.

28

And then almost more quickly than he believed possible, the days had passed and the long flight had been made, and the student of Thoth (Hermes) had been brought to a pause in the land of the pharaohs at the base of the Great Pyramid. Near him rose that solid guardian, the Sphinx, that great monument proclaiming the end of a former, more ancient age and the beginning of a new one.

He just stood and gazed upward that first day to where the Great Pyramid stood so firmly on its great bedrock of limestone, that rock of ages past. He had wondered how it would feel after the lapse of so much time, and he was a bit surprised at himself. It felt like yesterday, as if the earth had made a revolution or two and here he was again, where he belonged and, of all places on earth, where he felt most at home.

Perhaps he felt that way because of the several Egyptian lives he had led. He didn't know. Perhaps it was simply that it was here not so long ago really that he had made a choice, reached out for something, made a promise...In many ways he had come back to remember and to reaffirm that which seemed to have occurred only yesterday.

He spoke the names of the guardians, those two entities who had dedicated themselves to the preservation of the sanctity of the Pyramid thousands of years ago, who had offered to remain spirits on earth for as long as the Great Temple of God stood on the bedrock, as long as the Brotherhood remained as custodian of the records. And woe to those who come to desecrate and profane that for which the Brothers were responsible. The guardians were there to thwart foolishness and maliciousness. And when they had to, they reacted immediately.

Yehneh then stood on the road before the Sphinx staring up at the Pyramid. At the mention of their names the guardians moved outward to him. He told them he had come, that he was finally there. And they welcomed him. Then, when dismissed, they receded in space, unseen by all but Yehneh, fading like ghost images on a mirror back to the ancient recesses of the King's Chamber of the Great Pyramid, to continue their eternal vigil.

Yehneh wished to spend the night of the fourth within the King's Chamber of the Great Pyramid. He asked the Master and was told to seek permission from the local authorities to do so.

The morning of the third was spent visiting the offices of the various officers of the government. He was told everywhere he went in a friendly but firm fashion that what he desired to do was now impossible. Within the last year, the government had decided it was too much of a security risk to allow tourists, or anyone else, permission to spend nights in the Great Pyramid or any other national monument.

Yehneh was a little disappointed but he was told by the master that it necessary for him to ask permission to "physically" stay the night. It had been part of his vow to come back and to meet with the Brothers in the Pyramid. By attempting to gain permission for a physical stay, he had partially satisfied his vows.

In the afternoon of the same day, he returned to Giza and the Pyramid. He entered the structure with some tourists, who were numerous, and climbed the ramp leading to the Hall of Initiation, bent down and entered the King's Chamber. Around him were the unspoiled walls of the main initiation room. Before him was the black granite "sarcophagus," the seat of life that proclaimed the triumph of life over death. On the northwest side of the sarcophagus was the "waiting" stone. He sat and rested. It was very warm in the Chamber.

He leaned back and rested and listened to some of the remarks made by the tourists. So much of it was inaccurate, based on false myth, imagination and plain lies. Some of the things said profaned the sanctity of the place itself and all it stood for. He wondered if they would say the same things if they understood the significance of the initiation structure as a whole and of the particular room they were now in.

Then, during one of those rare brief periods when no tourists were about, he climbed into the sarcophagus, lay upon his back and prayed to God. He offered himself, his body, his life, his spirit to the Creator. He gave himself, his spirit, back to the Creator that He might do with him what He would have done. He offered himself completely to the Creator's service.

In his ears rang the peculiar booming that one heard as he lay in the sarcophagus. It was as if all the energy of the structure radiated to this one spot. This was the nexus, the living center. Here the Creator's Light Energy was focused.

Yehneh could ''hear'' the life of the place pulsating about him and through him. Lying in the sarcophagus, he became part of the sinew and spirit of his Father's House.

Finally he arose and left the Temple and returned to Cairo.

29

That night in the hotel room he prayed to God for guidance. He asked the Master if he should try to place consciously the exact spot of the buried archives, a thing he had never as yet tried to do, although he was always aware that his subconscious knew the place and that, God willing, he would remember at the right moment. He felt that now was the right moment. He had a great impulse to try, and the Master verified it for him and told him to proceed.

Yehneh had brought several books with him. Along with the Bible and the *Zohar*, he had Brother Doreal's translation of Thoth's *Emerald Tablets* and Mary Ellen Carter's *Edgar Cayce on*

Prophecy. He also had a map of the Sphinx and Great Pyramid area. All these he laid out before him.

Yehneh prayed again to God for guidance. He asked the Master to lead him to God's Will. He wanted to please God, and thereby to please the Master and the Brothers of the White Brotherhood—thus fulfilling his vow to return and to serve in his Father's name.

He opened Carter's work and read the words of Ra-Ta, High Priest to King Arart at the time of the building of the Sphinx, the secreting of the records and the raising of the Great Pyramid. In all of this, Ra-Ta had been instrumental, had supplied his inspiration and energy until his release from the physical. Then, in the twentieth century, he had returned as Edgar Cayce to help prepare the way for the greater understanding among all men before the sweeping earth changes which were necessary for the spiritual evolution of the present life wave.

This was the humble man of the twentieth century who ministered gratis and in the name of God to the sick in body and mind when he could be of assistance, and the same man who pointed out that the Great Pyramid was not only the record of the past but of "He who is to come": that is, the coming of Jesus the Christ, the returning of Christ. It is in the transcriptions of his "readings" that the meaning of the Great Pyramid as a monument to the glory of God, as an initiation Temple for those spiritually seeking, and as an indicator of the earth's future course, is voiced for those in the twentieth century who would listen. Cayce had come back to prepare the way.

Hugh Lynn Cayce also came back to prepare the way and to continue the work of his father, as have so many others in the Cayce family and those in intimate communion with it. As King Arart, Hugh Lynn Cayce had played a large organizational role in Khem, which later became the Egypt of the pharaohs. As Hugh Lynn Cayce in the twentieth century, he has never faltered in his devotion to the truths uttered in the "readings" and his desire to see the day when the records should break into the light to lead men more surely into the future. He has kept the Word sacred and kept his personal vows as well.

It was Hept Shupt, the old Atlantean priest, who had superintended the building of the Great Pyramid. It was Hept Shupt, Ra-Ta's good friend, who had talked the king into building the record chamber to protect the sacred archives being gathered in this new polyglot and polychrome land from Atlantis and elsewhere in the last days of Poseidia. Wise, capable and loving Hept Shupt who would become known to succeeding generations of "Egyptians" as Thoth, and later still as Hermes Trismegistis. The Hermetic Brotherhood would keep the Light burning and pass its flame throughout the known world. Later, as the world evolved spiritually, Moses and John the Baptist and Jesus would undergo final initiation in the Great Temple as have so many others. Jesus, soon to become Master Before All Masters when the Melchizedek spirit entered into Him (when the Logos or the Word descended, symbolized by the Dove-like Spirit descending upon Him as He is baptized by His Brother), would step forward to assume the Crown of Brotherhood, a being who was first among equals, as he had so long been even as Amelius in the androgynous age.

Yehneh, then as Threegee Sar Tana of Urfina, had been raised in the priest schools of Atlantis and had later immigrated to Khem (present-day Egypt) where he had been accepted as a priest and further indoctrinated into the Wisdom. He was trusted by both the Sons of the Law of One of Atlantis and by his new countrymen of Khem. Along with Horta, his friend Johnstone in the present life, he had been enlisted by Hept Shupt to supervise the transportation and burial of the sacred archives.

Johnstone had been Ra-Ta's most trusted priest. Yehneh and his friend had returned in this life to take part in what Yehneh felt was a great honor—to help raise what had remained so long in safekeeping, the history of the people.

Yehneh leaned back and read as Cayce had said, "This in position lies, as the sun rises from the waters, the line of the shadow (or light) falls between the paws of the Sphinx, that was later set as the sentinel or guard, and which may not be entered from the connecting chambers from the Sphinx's paw (right paw) until the time has been fulfilled when the charges must be active in this sphere of man's experience. Between, then, the Sphinx and the river.''

And then he took in his hand Brother Doreal's translation of the *Emerald Tablets* of Thoth and he read,

Then gathered I, the sons of Atlantis; into the spaceship I brought all my records, brought the records of sunken Atlantis; gathered I all of my powers, instruments many, of mighty magic.

Up then we rose on wings of the morning, high we arose above the Temple, leaving behind the Three and Dweller, deep in the Halls neath the Temple. Down neath the waves sank the Temple, closing the pathway to the Lords of the Cycles; yet ever to him, who has knowing, open shall be the path to Amenti.

Fast fled we then, on the wings of the morning, fled to the land of the children of Khem. There by my power I conquered and ruled them, raised I to Light the children of Kehm.

Deep neath the rocks, I buried my spaceship, waiting the time when man might be free. Over the spaceship, erected a marker in the form of a lion, yet like unto man; there neath the image rests, yet, my spaceship, forth to be brought when need shall arise.

Know ye, O man, that far in the future, invaders shall come from out of the deep; then awake, ye who have wisdom, bring forth my ship and conquer with ease.

Deep neath the image lies my secret, search and find in the pyramid I built. Each to the other, is the Keystone: each the gateway, that leads into Life. Follow the key I leave behind me, seek and the doorway to Life shall be thine. Seek thou in my pyramid, deep in the passage that ends in a wall, use thou the Key of the Seven, and open to thee, the pathway will fall.

Now, unto thee I have given my wisdom, now unto thee, I have given my way; follow the pathway, solve thou my secrets, unto thee I have shown the way.

There Yehneh could see was explained the sacred connection between the Sphinx and the Great Initiation Temple, the Great Pyramid. "The passage that ends in a wall" referred to the bottom of the initiation chamber, or well, in the Pyramid. The Key of the Seven referred to the planets, their forceful fields and especially to the Council of Seven Govenors of the solar system. It also referred to the Seven Fingers of Ra-Ta. A symbol, of course, is something that stands for something else. The Brotherhood had long ago adopted a symbolic technique as a safeguard against misuse of knowledge that not everyone was ready for with the understanding that, when the time was right, that symbolic knowledge would be made clear. Yehneh turned the pages of the *Emerald Tablets* and read,

Now shall I speak of thee of knowledge, ancient beyond the thought of thy race. Know ye that we of the Great Race had, and have knowledge, that is more than man's. Wisdom we gained from the star-born races, wisdom and knowledge far beyond man's. Down to us had descended masters of wisdom, as far beyond us as I am from thee. List ye, now while I give ye wisdom, use it and free shalt thou be.

Know ye that in the pyramid I builded are the KEYS that shall show ye the WAY into life; aye, draw ye a line from the great image, I builded, to the apex of the pyramid, built as a gateway. draw ye another opposite in the same angle and direction, dig ye and find that which I have hidden. There shall ye find the underground entrance, to the secrets hidden before ye were man.

Yehneh took a pencil and, using the edge of a book for a ruler, drew a line from a spot in the middle of the beginning of the right paw of the Sphinx to the apex of the Pyramid. Then for a moment he hesitated. What did "another opposite in the same angle and direction" mean? Opposite to what?

He prayed to God for guidance in the name of the Master Before All Masters, also in the name of Thoth, in the name of the White Brotherhood and the Hermetic Brotherhood and in the name of all those who seek God and need Him. Then he drew a line from the spot in the middle of the beginning of the right paw at the same angle to a spot directly in front of the Great Pyramid and the same distance from the "middle spot" as the "middle spot" was from the Pyramid's apex. That made a ninety degree angle at the "middle spot" where the two lines joined.

He then split the ninety degree angle with a line going due north, parallel to the base of the Great Pyramid. Then a line from the apex of the Pyramid until it intersected the north running line parallel to the Pyramid's base. That series of lines made a pyramid.

Then Yehneh drew a line connecting the right base of this pyramid to the line that ended at this moment in space directly before the Pyramid. That completed another pyramid, an inverted one. For an instant, Yehneh was not sure if the sacred archives were buried at point A or point B. He prayed again to God for assistance. (See map.)

Yehneh glanced at the *Emerald Tablets*, and the first thing his eyes saw was the subheading of Tablet XI that read "THE KEY TO ABOVE AND BELOW" and immediately he knew. He was sure. It was point B.

As things are in the "higher" planes, so they are below on the earth plane. The Creator's cosmic laws are consistent and immutable. That ancient wisdom had been drafted into the very chambers that now housed the sacred archives. From ABOVE, the top of the Great Pyramid, Temple of Initiation, whereupon the mount is set the stone offering table (called a "hotep") to BELOW, where the buried archives recording the history of the sojourn on this planet of the Creator's people are found, the balance of God's creation is announced and made manifest.

Those records, buried facing the

East, the birth, the new day, are one of the vehicles of experience man must find the will to use, if he is to develop more quickly and rise upward into the "higher" planes of greater experience. The Creator through the Elder Brothers will show the way to a new day if only we will follow.

Yehneh thanked God and then slept the sleep of the contented.

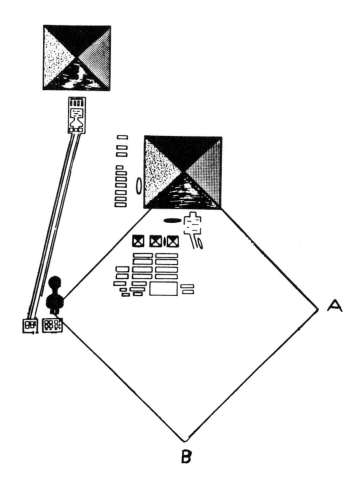

30

The next day Yehneh walked about Cairo listening to the sounds and watching the shifting images of the busy city. He did not go to Giza and the Pyramid. He came back to his hotel room and rested.

That evening he read and rested. He remembered that Venus was in conjunction with the moon as was Neptune. At midnight, the morning of the fifth, they would be in conjunction with each other. Cosmically that was important. He had planned to astrally project himself to the King's Chamber of the Great Pyramid at midnight of the fifth. He knew there was an initiatory ceremony he must attend. It was part of the vow he had made long ago, and he intended to keep it as best he could.

The initiation was very necessary as far as the project was concerned. Edgar Cayce had accurately said that the record tomb could not be entered without an understanding. The guardians could not be passed until after the seekers had been regenerated on the Mount of the Pyramid.

He started to prepare for bed shortly before midnight. He turned out the lights and lay for a while in the dark. He prayed and closed his eyes but he was not at all sleepy.

He decided to switch the light back on. Something was wrong.

He spoke to the Master. Was he doing what he should? Should he even now be at the Great Temple?

He was told to project himself. The time was now. Not the evening of the fifth. Now.

He lay with a pillow behind his back, propped up against the headboard of the bed. He was very excited and worried whether he could achieve a very deep trance state with such a high degree of excitement.

He prayed for help. Then he began the relaxation exercises as usual, starting at his toes and finally culminating at the top of his head. Then he began the rhythmic movement of his etheric energy between his pineal eye and pituitary region. Back and forth, to and fro, "Ro-da, Ro-da, Ro-da," he intoned. He was doing everything a bit different from before. He had never used that combination of words, that he could remember. But they seemed right. They came out of his subconscious into his mouth like artesian waters rising from unknown depths. They happened by themselves.

Finally, as he intuited that the proper rhythmic rate had been reached, he commanded his etheric body away, flung it out into the ether, directing it toward the Great Temple.

His astral body was projected to the King's Chamber. He entered and greeted his Brothers and the two guardians who were awaiting him. They came forward to him as shadows, extending their hands, greeting him warmly. He shook their hands, and the affection that filled him was great.

Then he levitated himself in the sarcophagus, his head pointing north. The old Master N stepped forward and elevated his extended form higher, slightly above the sarcophagus. The Master began wrapping his body in the winding sheets of the dead, round and round about him from the neck downward, thus symbolizing the death of the body.

He heard his Brothers begin to chant "Horem, Horem, Horem, Horem, Horem...." For an instant, his mind started, "What are they saying?" but before the words passed his lips, he knew the answer. "Why, of course, they are saying 'Horus, Horus.' They are calling to Horus."

Thus Yehneh's spirit was sent to his Creator, out of the ark to the bosom of God, keeping the covenant long ago given to His human creation. At that moment he gave himself back to his Creator, so that he might be reborn in Him again. He understood that at that instant of absorption, he became Horus (The Word, the Logos, the Medchizedek Spirit); he became Yehneh Horem, born again in

God. Yehneh knew that the names of deity might change with time and from culture to culture but the principle remained eternal.

Then the Master N anointed his brow and his mouth, consecrating this reborn spirit to the Creator in New Life. He then unbound the body as it symbolically and literally came forth into the light of a new day.

Yehneh then removed himself from the sarcophagus that has stood twelve thousand years in the Great Temple, and long before that in Atlantis, as a symbol that there is no death of the seeking soul that is not followed by a rebirth. He was again greeted by his Brothers, and he warmly embraced the Master N. They stood and held each other in their arms, and Yehneh felt the Master patting him on his back. He loved the Master N, loved them all more than words can tell.

Then Yehneh sat down on the "waiting" stone, beside the sarcophagus, and rested. But almost before he was seated, there appeared at the entrance a Great Light.

And the Light looked at the Master

N, and at all of them, and said that the Creator was pleased. How Yehneh's spirit soared with those words! The Light indicated the old Master N and said the Creator wished for him and, looking then to Yehneh, the scribe to continue to raise the records. Yehneh kept thinking that he should be standing out of respect for the Light, but he seemed rooted in awe and admiration to the very spot, as if he himself were part of the stone.

Thus was that night the ancient ritual of life replayed, as it had been twelve thousand years ago and is even so to this day. Thus was the promise kept, because of the love of the Light and the enternal forgiving guidance of God.

31

So it is that the "KEY of the SEVEN" of which Thoth, that great servant of God and of mankind, spoke was used by his student, Yehneh, who does love him greatly.

On the morning of the sixth Mercury (Thoth's own) conjuncted with the moon, as if to seal the endeavor, and a new moon appeared in the skies, a symbol not only of Yehneh's initiation but a harbinger of those initiations to come to all those who seek.

The seventh day brought the conjunction of Mars and the moon. This added a positive note of energy and persistence to the unfoldment of the cosmic course of things.

Now let it be seen that seven planets did conjunct in seven days, starting with the conjunction of Jupiter and Saturn on the night of December 31, 1980 and ending with the conjunction of Mars and the moon on January 7, 1981. During that time Yehneh's ruling planet, Venus, was conjuncted by Neptune, placed in his twelfth house. It was a time of remembering and a time of religious insight—a propitious moment that was to be.

The afternoon of the seventh, Yehneh sat on the bed in his hotel room in Cairo and wrote the Statement and the Agreement which was dictated to him through the Master, his guide, in the name of the Creator and the White Brotherhood, and which was to be sent to the appropriate parties, so that the records might now, in that ancient phrase, come out into the light of day.

AGREEMENT

The White Brotherhood, Order of Melchizedek, in the name of the Father and His Son, Master Before All Masters, the Christ, releases to the world the ancient records of the sacred archives of the Temple at Giza which was built to the Glory of God and His Living Spirit in anticipation of the return of the Master. The White Brotherhood has been privileged to serve as guardian-keeper of these records for many centuries and has hopefully awaited the moment when all men everywhere would once again claim the knowledge which is their heritage and is their birthright. These, then, are the records of the past, collected and protected by the Thoth-Christ Spirit which is One, with the knowledge that men of this day will grow in the Spirit of God in the future, by looking at that which has been. All is initimately One. As above, so below. So must it be.

It is agreed that:

The Association of Research and Enlightenment will be given the exact location of the sacred archives by the White Brotherhood, in the name of Jesus who became the Christ, Master

Before All Masters, on this day
_____.

The Association for Research and Enlightenment will show evidence within one year's time that it is making an effort to excavate the site wherein the archives are buried. If the Association for Research and Enlightenment has not shown an effort at retrieval within one year, the information concerning the location will be given to other agencies so that the wish of the Masters will be accomplished.

The Association for Research and Enlightenment will receive from the White Brotherhood in the name of Christ, Master Before All Masters, within six months of this day _____ a manuscript describing the finding of the sacred archives. The Association will have, after receiving the manuscript, six months from that day within which to agree to publish it. At the end of six months the manuscript will be published elsewhere.

The White Brotherhood wishes that all monies collected from publication of this manuscript and any monies raised collectively because of activities involved in recovering the sacred archives be set aside in a separate account to be administered by the Association for Research and Enlightenment in conjunction with the White Brotherhood. This account may be used for expenses arising from travel, excavation, restoration, preservation and dissemination of the records and for those purposes only.

It is the wish of the White Brotherhood that no individual receive personal financial gain from the sacred archives.

It is the desire of the White Brotherhood that the name(s) of the messenger(s) of the Brotherhood be kept confidential.

It is especially the wish of the White Brotherhood that the historical information contained in the sacred archives be disseminated as broadly and as quickly as possible across the world.

Therefore, by the excavation of the information in the sacred archives and its dissemination worldwide, the White Brotherhood is assured that those who read directly and those who hear of the information contained in the archives will have a greater appreciation of world brotherhood and a greater knowledge of the One God's loving Spirit as is sent to mankind through His Shepherd, the loving Master Before All Masters, Jesus, the most worthy man who became the Christ. So must it be.

32

Then Yehneh traveled north to the old city of Thebes, now called Luxor. And he traveled into the Gorna Mountains on the back of a donkey as he had done many lifetimes ago. He saw the tombs of the pharaohs and their queens and the loyal lords of those days. It was a returning to times that were dear to him, and he was greatly moved by what he saw.

At the Temple of Seti I he met a man that had been a father to him in the reign of that pharaoh. They embraced and held each other closely, and when he left, the man was close to tears. Yehneh could see the man did not understand himself, and Yehneh wished he could explain to him the wondrous truth. But he did not. It was not the right time. Subconsciously, the man did understand. For now, Yehneh knew, that must be enough. Love had met love and remembered, as it always does.

And then he and his guide continued on into the mountains, and the sun shone bright with the white light, glinting about and glazing the sharp rocks, roasting out the dry truth of things and exposing it to the light of day. It was not a place where shadows made their abode.

Yehneh had a lot of time, traveling lazily through the heat of the day, to think over what had happened to him during the previous eight days at the Great Temple in Giza and in Cairo. All that seemed so wondrous, and yet he knew it was all as true and as real as the sharp stones about him, actually truer, because things of the spirit outlast the firmest limestone rock and hardest chip of chert. Only spirit endures forever.

During the twelve thousand years since the burial of the sacred archives much stone had passed to sand. Over the earth, mountain ranges had risen in places that had been quite flat. Vast reaches of the earth's crust were now covered with water. Once they had been heavily populated areas thriving with human life. Rivers had ceased to run that had flowed without interruption for millennia and now were waterless wastes. And waterless wastes had greened, becomes oases on the face of the earth, supporting millions of living, developing people. Even the Nile in that most unchanging part of the world had shifted her course a little.

Thus did the life waves shift with the cosmic tides. And so it would be in the future. Change is fundamental to cosmic law, there can be no doubt. As the planet revolves in its cycle, it continues rushing outward into the cosmic ether, our galaxy and others like it opening outward like the petals of a great lotus, coming to new flower perpetually, into time that is no time, with speed that is no speed, part of all that is growing, enlarging itself in His Own Grand Plan, the ultimate flowering of God's Creation.

Yehneh realized now that so long as we yearn to grow in spirit, which only endures, the Creator will continue to give us our opportunities on earth and elsewhere to grow in His Image. He who seeks will surely find. To him who knocks, it shall be opened, said the Christ. That is the beginning without end that the searching soul will find.

Yehneh recalled the words of Thoth in the *Emerald Tablets*, "In every land form ye the mysteries, make the way hard for the seeker to tread. Thus will the weak and wavering be rejected, thus will the secrets be hidden and guarded, held till the time when the wheel shall be turned."

And now, Yehneh knew, the wheel was about to be turned decisively. The world continually changes both spiritually and physically. Usually, however, these changes are almost imperceptible to the average person. Ever so often, God's Living Instruments including the Elder Brothers, responding to the Creator's Word, redirect the flow of spiritual and physical energies in patterns that become obviously perceptible. And such will be especially the case the next forty years.

Those who seek during this time to understand their human past will be the wiser for it—if they learn from the mistakes of that past. And thus they will grow in spirit more quickly.

The Elder Brothers wish the sacred archives of Thoth to be made available to all. These are the records of the people. They belong to them as signposts along the way. They are just that much more evidence of the Creator's Will, that Will which we mortals seem so often to forget. Paul says "know ye not that ye are Gods?" If we are to become "God-men in truth as in essence ye be," as Thoth has written, then we had best remember the lessons of our past experiences on earth so that we may grow the better.

Mortal man must claim his divine heritage. His God awaits the proper recognition. He wishes to be met with that Love which He so freely gives. Prodigal sons begin to grow spiritually when they cease being egocentered creatures and listen to the spark of the Creator that burns with White Light within them and will guide them, if only they will let it.

Jehovah, one of the leaders of the Elohim, says to Ezekiel, "They and their fathers have transgressed against me, even unto this day." He is not very optimistic that they will listen to his messenger's message. "The house of Israel will not hearken unto thee; for they will not hearken unto me.'' Yet Jehovah tells him to proceed that ''they shall know that there hath been a prophet among them.'' Yehneh knew now that to hear the prophets and to understand, one had to understand one's own self first.

Yehneh stopped on the high sharp cliff overlooking the Nile Valley. He thought of all that had happened to him—how far he had personally come in distance and in understanding. He could smile a bit when he remembered how willing he had been to sell his soul, give away the spark of life in him to negative forces in the mistaken idea he was sacrificing himself and his friend to ''free'' the records. How clumsily vain and misdirected that had been, and how short a time ago that had been. He now knew how far the path stretched out before him, and he could not even yet begin to see the end of it, and yet look how far he had come in such a short time, once he began to see more clearly. He knew now how quickly men can change their lives and learn to see, insist on seeing through using the spiritual spark of God within them. That is the Light which ultimately leads us all and is our salvation.

Yehneh realized that those who were willing to see would grow more quickly, flower to perfection sooner as did the lotus below him in the fertile life-supporting backwaters of the Nile. They would save themselves much grief, much hard learning in the times ahead. He knew how loving was the Creator of all—and how forgiving. Had not God, after all his mistakes, said "Let nothing put asunder that which I have made whole again?" He knew well now how God could heal. He knew that a soul had to give itself to God completely, to be shaped as the Creator would have it. That was the only way. And it was not a "sacrifice" at all but a rebirth into immortal life.

Let us hope, then, that all the people everywhere on earth will soon acknowledge the spark of Light that is the Godhead within them. Then they will know that they are truly Brothers, inseparable within the Creator, who promised through Jehovah that "I will give them one heart, and I will put a new spirit within you..." for "they shall be my people, and I will be their God.'' So it is meant to be finally for all God's children. As it is above, so surely must it be below. As the children of Ham say today in the ancient land of Khem—*Inshalla*. Whatever God's will.

33

Yehneh returned home and wrote up a report of his trip and experiences. Then he contacted Hugh Lynn Cayce and arranged to meet with him and present the report to him personally. In his mind, he could not help but wonder why Mr. Cayce had not contacted him in December. His feelings were, if he were to be completely honest with himself, a little hurt.

He arrived in Virginia Beach and was greeted warmly by Mr. Cayce, which immediately made him feel better. When Mr. Cayce told him that he had wanted to make the trip with him but was too sick to do so, Yehneh felt better but a little ashamed that he had thought the worst—that perhaps he was not interested in pursuing the project with him.

Then Yehneh recalled that Mr. Cayce had lost one kidney to disease and it now appeared the other was dysfunctional as well. In fact, the opposite of his worst thoughts seemed to have been the case. Hugh Lynn Cayce thanked him for the manuscript and they parted amicably. And Yehneh flew back to Chicago to await Mr. Cayce's reaction to his report.

He waited and waited and nothing happened. Weeks went by, several months. Still no word. When he tried to get hold of him by telephone, he was told Mr. Cayce was out of town, which wasn't unusual because Hugh Lynn Cayce traveled for the Association for Research and Enlightenment a great deal. This, however, did not make Yehneh feel much better, although it was something to fall back on for awhile.

Then one morning thunder struck. He opened his newspaper to read that Hugh Lynn Cayce was dead. His weakened body had finally failed him.

Yehneh, in spite of his best efforts and the advice of his guide, became deeply depressed. Gradually he began to feel that he had failed the Brotherhood and most of all himself. He couldn't help it. The more he tried to think positively, the more he seemed to slip downward.

As the months and years passed, and with the good coaching of his guide, he began to put things in better perspective. He had, after all, overcome much, self-doubts, some serious vanity problems and Johnstone's disillusionment with the project. He had, after all, made the journey. He had located the spot, had projected to the King's Chamber and offered his soul to God surrounded by the happy astral projections of his Brothers. How fortunate to have been given the opportunity. How blessed, he realized, to have been found worthy enough for the venture. He began to hold his head up a little higher. Finally, he began to smile inwardly at himself. How misdirected of him, he thought, to think he had failed when one considered all he had been given. He knew how patient his guide had been with him. He could only imagine and marvel at how patient God Himself must be.

It encouraged him even more to read

in the newspaper one morning that a villager, living in the squatter settlement almost directly in front of the Sphinx, had unearthed a temple of Thoth while digging by his home. It was very close to the spot Yehneh had triangulated that night in his hotel room in Cairo. The news didn't surprise him at all. He knew this was an indication that the ancient Egyptians had later built, almost predictably, a whole complex of temples and buildings yet undiscovered in the immediate vicinity of where the record shaft had been secretly bored.

But sometimes when the days began to drag a little, and time seemed almost to stop—sometimes late at night when everything was so quiet you could hear your heart beat, Yehneh would begin to daydream about the Lost Pyramid. He wondered who it would be who would finally raise the records to the light of day. Would it be some virtuous Percival among men who had yet to make his appearance, someone more faultless than he? Or would it be some flawed Lancelot who, at last finding a greater perfection in himself, would come to the rescue and raise up the story of ancient man, more ancient than most men dare dream? Who would be so bold? he wondered. And who so worthy as to succeed?

EXTRATERRESTRIALS IN BIBLICAL PROPHECY
and the New Age Great Experiment
G. Cope Schellhorn

Now the greater truth emerges. Professor Schellhorn has skillfully demonstrated the large body of evidence that suggests extraterrestrial visitors have long been occupied with visiting our planet, biologically engineering the development of man and directing certain control cultures such as the early Hebrews. Using his own research and new evidence from scholars involved in Near Eastern Studies, he uncovers the forgotten meaning of certain key biblical words that prove incontestably that the extraterrestrials mated with early man and continued their involvement with mankind in a "Great Experiment" that is still continuing today. The return of a Messiah "out of the clouds" is not metaphor but fact—and the Messiah's "army of heaven" is not only truly extraterrestrial but has been here before. Amazingly, one cause of the catastrophic earth changes prophesied to occur during "end times" and mentioned in the Book of Revelation was known to the ancient Sumerians and Babylonians—"Wormwood." But the Babylonians knew it was the planet Marduk and its satellites and calculated its return. Thus mankind will soon be tested in trials by fire—with the promise of scripture that the Messiah and his extraterrestrial host will be standing by to offer assistance to those who will listen.

430 pages. Illustrated.